Memoirs of Normalcy

Journey from Sedentary to Extraordinary

Joleene DesRosiers Moody

BALBOA.
PRESS

A DIVISION OF HAY HOUSE

Balboa Press books may be ordered through booksellers or by contacting:

Balboa Press
A Division of Hay House
1663 Liberty Drive
Bloomington, IN 47403
www.balboapress.com
1-(877) 407-4847

Because of the dynamic nature of the Internet, any web addresses or links contained in this book may have changed since publication and may no longer be valid. The views expressed in this work are solely those of the author and do not necessarily reflect the views of the publisher, and the publisher hereby disclaims any responsibility for them.

The author of this book does not dispense medical advice or prescribe the use of any technique as a form of treatment for physical, emotional, or medical problems without the advice of a physician, either directly or indirectly. The intent of the author is only to offer information of a general nature to help you in your quest for emotional and spiritual well-being. In the event you use any of the information in this book for yourself, which is your constitutional right, the author and the publisher assume no responsibility for your actions.

Some individual's names and identifying details have been changed to protect their privacy.

Print information is available on the last page.

ISBN: 978-1-4525-4568-4 (sc)
ISBN: 978-1-4525-4567-7 (e)
Library of Congress Control Number: 2012901440
Balboa Press rev. date: 4/7/2015

This book is dedicated to my mother, my husband and my daughter. Without any of you, I wouldn't be who I am today. Mom, I miss you and wish you were here. Mark, you are my love, my life, my happiness. Thanks to your loving kindness, you have made all things possible. And Maddie, you are, by far, the *best* thing that has ever happened to me. To all of you: I am grateful for your love and patience and forever will be.

Contents

Part 1: The Journey

Part 2: Do Something Different

Preface

If you picked up this book because you feel lost or stuck or are in need of change, don't put it down. I realize there are lots of books out there that promise change in two weeks if you follow "these simple step-by-step instructions." I can't offer that to you. And I wont. I don't believe there exists what is known as instant gratification. There is no book or workshop or television show that will change your life in five days or less. Everybody is different. And everybody must experience change on a different level with different means and tools. My goal is to make the journey of change personally enriching; to share stories from people like you and me that will help you come to your own conclusion on how to make change based on your own personal experiences. Yes, I will ask you to pose questions to yourself or consider doing something crazy (like getting in your car and purposely getting lost so you can find your way back in an effort to prove to yourself that you *can* find your way back), and yes, I will make you think as you begin to understand that your flaws are as prevalent and revealing as my flaws or your brother's flaws or your husband's or wife's flaws or your mother's flaws and blah, blah, blah. I will even ask you to take inventory of what you have now and what you want today to help you grow. We'll talk about what you want to change and why you want to change it. I will be whoever you need me to be as you read. I'll be your best friend or your sister or your coworker. I can be your mother or your brother or your aunt. I'm not overly particular. As long as I've had breakfast and I look halfway decent, I'll be that person. Bear in mind that the suggestions I pose in this book are just that - suggestions. Do with them what you like. Don't get me wrong, books and workshops are a fantastic way to move you through any change process. Quite frankly, I encourage you to read as many books as you can or attend a workshop in your area. Just bear in mind that they are tools; ever flowing reminders of what we need to do to create a better life for ourselves and ultimately, for those around us.

Memoirs of Normalcy is a journey, really. Your very own journey. As you move forward with any change you make you'll recognize that what you're doing is very normal. You'll recall instances where you did something that you thought was crazy or out of the ordinary and shouldn't be considered normal. I challenge you to rethink that. There isn't much in this world that should be considered out of the ordinary. Ever.

I chose the title *Memoirs of Normalcy* because this book is also a memoir of my own journey – a journey made up of lots of adventures and continual growing. Change doesn't need to be difficult or painful or daunting, regardless of what others have told you. When you understand that it truly is a journey with lots of interesting and unexpected twists and turns, you'll begin to open your mind to a life that is all yours to play with and mold. Yes, you'll have down days. Even the Dalai Lama has days where his energy is low. One day you'll think you have a handle on things and the next day you'll feel lost again. That's the way it's supposed to be – at least for a little while. If you reach full enlightenment in thirty days or less, call me. I want to bottle what you have and sell it to the world.

You should know that it isn't always easy to make certain changes. Some will go more smoothly than others. And that's because we do what we are conditioned to do so very well. We get up, go to work, come home, make a meal and go to bed. Routines keep life simple. Once we change our routine to invite new experiences or a new understanding of our lives and the world around us, our brain will fight us. We are so locked into the cultural belief that change is complicated, that we don't think it's possible to change careers or leave toxic relationships or lose weight or feel anything but constantly depressed. We tell ourselves, "This is the way it's supposed to be." We become afraid. Dr. Wayne Dyer says it best with one little sentence: "Turn fear into curiosity." And believe it or not, it can be done.

Oh. One more thing. I am one of those people who thrive on quotes of greatness. Too often we forget the simplicity of life and how to love. I'm often guilty of this, so I like to remind myself with words of wisdom. You will see a quote above each chapter that is related to the content of the chapter. I think it sets the tone of what you're about to read and gives you a deeper insight as how spiritual and very moving your transformation can and will be. I also refer to God and the Universe in several different ways. They are one and the same. Depending on your faith, you may remove whatever word I use and replace it with what makes you comfortable.

So what do you say? Would you like to take a journey of reinvention with me?

Good. I was hoping you'd say yes.

Part 1:

The Journey

Chapter 1:

A short story.

"Choose Growth over fear." – Elizabeth Lesser

I need to begin with a little story before we get into anything else because it's the entire reason I wrote this book. If I start throwing all sorts of words and ideas at you without you knowing where they come from, you may not see the authenticity of who I am or what I'm trying to say. And it's important that you do see my authenticity. I write these words as a humble human being, equal to each and every person on this planet. I am equal to you and to your children and your spouse and your best friend; equal to Charlie Sheen and Lindsay Lohan and President Obama and Lady Gaga. There is no one person on this planet greater or better than another. We are all made of the same matter and energy and we all come from the same source. We are all beautiful in our own skin, big or small. The knowledge I offer is nothing new. It has been shared through sermons, books, and indigenous peoples for hundreds and hundreds of years. But I digress - which is often the case - so here's the story.

1

I used to be a television reporter in Upstate New York. I wasn't the best, but I was pretty darn good. I won a few awards and even had the privilege of appearing on an episode of *Snapped* on the Oxygen network after I covered a trial that gained national attention. I graduated from a field reporter to a fill-in anchor and as far as those watching me from their living rooms were concerned, my life looked shiny and sparkly and perfect. But it wasn't. I was very unhappy. I didn't like what I did for a living. I liked where I worked and most of the people I worked with, but I didn't necessarily enjoy what I did. And I drank a lot because of it. I dreaded getting up every morning. I put great fear in front of me as I drove into the city of Syracuse day after day. What story would I be covering? Would I do it successfully? Who would I have to call and bother to get more information? Would I meet my deadline? What would the other stations produce? Would their story be better than my story? At the time I thought I played this question game with myself because I wanted to be the best. I wanted to be recognized as a *damn good* reporter. Now I realize it was because I simply didn't enjoy what I was doing. I was miserable. I hated calling people and pestering them for an interview. More than that, I loathed showing up on their doorstep, especially when a mother who had just lost her child in an accident was on the other side of the door.

If I truly loved what I was doing, I wouldn't feel that way. Instead, every fiber of my being would light up. I would enjoy going to work. I would look forward to tackling my assignments. But that just wasn't the case. I felt dead inside. Nothing lit up for me. I wanted more. I needed healthier challenges and a clearer avenue. It was time for change. And I knew it. I just didn't know how to get there.

And then one day my brother called me with news that would change the way I looked at my body and soul forever. It would reshape and redefine the meaning of my life, forcing me to color it with new crayons and put it in a completely different perspective.

It was a hot Saturday in August of 2009. I was sitting on the front porch of my two-bedroom apartment smoking a cigarette and drinking a beer. I had just finished cleaning my house and was thinking about how lonely I felt with no one to love and share the day with. My daughter was with her father and I had just left yet another failing relationship and was awfully busy feeling sorry for myself. All of that self-pity disappeared when my big brother called and told me my mother's husband found her dead in their bed. She suffered from chronic obstructive pulmonary disease (COPD) and lived with an oxygen tube up her nose. Apparently her husband was out mowing the lawn on that very hot day. When he came back in to check on her, he said he found her lifeless. The doctor told us later she died peacefully in her sleep. I wasn't so sure. I imagined her gasping desperately for air, dying frightened and helpless as she tried to call out his name. She was sixty years old when she left this world.

The months that followed without her were easier than I would have imagined. I seemed to deal with grieving fairly easily. I remember thinking that too, that handling her death wasn't so bad. What I didn't know was that grieving is different for everybody. Some experience what is known as delayed mourning and that was apparently what was happening with me, because eight months after she died it hit me – and it hit me *hard*. I woke up every night for weeks sobbing relentlessly. I thought about the end of her life and how miserable she must have been. The kitchen counter in her house was full of pills (both prescribed and natural supplements) that she took in an attempt to rewind the damage she had done from years of smoking. The week after she died my brother and I scooped dozens of those bottles from the counter into a garbage bag. A spare bedroom in the back of the house was home to at least ten oxygen tanks and other machinery used to keep her breathing steady while she was still alive. I would think about how she could barely walk three feet without stopping, panting for breath and demanding that I, my brother or her husband get her a glass of water or a tissue. Thinking of how she suffered bothered me. But more than that, the part that killed me the most, was the fact that her husband buried her tiny box of ashes - *without ever telling us.* My brother and I went to the house one afternoon to pick up some things and I noticed her ashes weren't on the table in the living room. When I asked her husband where they were, he told me he had buried them. I can't even begin to tell you how angry and sad and shocked I was. In my mind, I felt he dumped her on the side of the road like a piece of garbage. And that troubled me for weeks.

As the rain pounded on my roof in the middle of the night, I would imagine her little box of ashes in the ground with her inside, cold and forgotten, and it would rip my heart out. All I could do was sob. Until one day I woke up and decided I couldn't take it anymore. The pain was more than I understood it to be. And not just because she was gone, but because I was experiencing an awakening in the light of her death that I didn't understand. I wanted to understand. I needed to understand. That meant I wasn't going to work that day. And so I didn't.

Now I should mention that shortly after my mother passed, I got to know a really wonderful man and we started a quiet relationship. Mark was as much of a train wreck as I was, which is probably why we got along so well. So when I told him that morning that I didn't want to go to work because my mind was "full", he understood completely. He kissed me goodbye and headed out the door to waddle through the ever-growing and often complicated world of the criminal justice system. Mark is a prosecutor.

I spent the day in angst, contemplating my life and rubbing my chest where my heart is. I hurt. I was confused. I had no idea where I was supposed to be or what I was supposed to be doing. I sat in the chair in front of my computer looking through the want ads with zero motivation. I didn't want another mundane job inside the walls of a building with partitions between the desks and animosity among the workers. I wanted to feel alive and full of purpose. I wanted to feel passion for my job and enjoy positive challenges. I wanted to live life like I had never lived it before, taking risks that could catapult me to a place I'd only dreamed of but never dared to go.

I knew that night as I pulled the covers up over my chin that I wasn't going to work the next day, either. Mark figured out my plan the following morning when I didn't head downstairs to beat him into the shower. I stayed in bed, my eyes fixated on the ceiling. I listened as he buzzed around downstairs, getting ready for his day. Soon he came upstairs and sat next to me on the bed.

"You staying home today?" he asked me.

I nodded.

"Do you plan on ever going back?" He said kiddingly as he pushed my hair off my forehead.

"I have to at some point. But not today."

He smiled and gently kissed me goodbye, leaving me in a cloud of contemplation lined with deep confusion.

The house was quiet. I felt very alone and very scared. I wondered if other people I knew felt like this. Was I the only one suffering this kind of angst? Who else in the world, at this very moment, was hiding under their covers not wanting to go to work? And how long have they been hiding? A week? A month? A *year?*

I dated a guy once that hated his job. *Hated* it. He was the bass player in a band I used to sing with. He worked six days a week, by choice, in a factory putting together car parts on an assembly line. This man was divorced with four kids and said he worked almost every day because he needed the money. One night after a show, we sat at the bar and he told me he was fortunate enough to have an ex-wife that didn't ask for alimony or child support. But she racked up so many bills when they were married, he said, that he was forced to work long hours to pay down the debt.

"How do you do it if you hate it so much?" I asked.

"Money talks," he said. "I get double time and a half working on Sundays. I can't say no to that."

"I dunno," I said taking a swig of my beer. "If I didn't like being someplace, I sure as hell wouldn't spend anymore time there than I needed to."

He nodded. I figured he had to be knee deep in debt to suffer going there six days a week.

"I suppose that's why I'm miserable," he said. "I can't go anywhere else. Where am I gonna go?"

He was significantly older than me, sporting a life of hard work that spawned heartache, a broken marriage and a less-than-stellar abode. But he had an amazing heart. I remember hoping I'd never end up in his situation. And if I ever did, I would fight like hell to get out of it.

I suddenly realized, as I lay there scared and practically motionless in my bed, that I had a very real decision to make. Do I stay in a place doing what I don't enjoy - or do I leave, so I can grow?

Even if everything seemed fuzzy one thing was clear: I was unhappy and I wanted out. I didn't want to go through another day feeling this way. You know the old cliché *life is too short?* Well it's true. Those used to be just words to me, but now I understood them – *really* understood them. What I heard as that little phrase echoed through my corroded brain that morning was: *It's time to move on. You're not doing what makes you happy and therefore you're not living to your full potential. Life is too short to wait any longer.*

I decided in that very moment that I wasn't going back to work. I'm sorry, but I just couldn't. On so many levels that I can't even begin to explain, I experienced absolutely no joy when I walked through those doors. As far as I was concerned, I shouldn't have to tolerate that feeling. Nobody should.

I yanked the covers off of me and wandered into our home office. I sat down and stared at my phone with tears in my eyes. And then I did something that I was very afraid to do: I called my supervisor and told him that something was very wrong with me – and that I needed to process whatever it was before I could effectively come back to work. I could tell he wasn't happy with what I was saying, but I really felt I had to be honest. I needed to take time to breathe and think. I had a huge decision to make and it wasn't going to come easy.

I spent the next four weeks out of work, living each day in a haze of pain and frustration. And I cried, too, every day. I cried everyday for hours, sometimes. Every afternoon that didn't bring rain, I would go for a walk through the open and empty field across from our little rental house and look to the sky begging for answers.

What am I supposed to be doing? What is my life purpose? What am I doing wrong and how do I right it? Please show me the way. Show me the way.

I would pray to a God I couldn't define, asking for answers to guide me in my confusion. And then I would apologize, asking that I not be forsaken just because I wasn't sure of who or what "He" was.

Two general thoughts plagued me as I wandered through those fields: The first was the reality behind my turmoil, which included the need to feed my daughter, pay my bills and fulfill all of the responsibilities that come with being an adult. The second was the guilt I carried because I *had* a job. In 2009 and 2010, hundreds of people were losing their jobs or getting laid off thanks to high oil prices and drama between the democrats and republicans in Washington. The result was a tanked economy and plenty of unrest with voters. There were people out there that would *kill* to have a job. And here I was whining because I didn't want mine anymore. I knew I just couldn't quit, not without a plan, anyway. Demons stalked me at night, taunting my decisions and laughing at my demise. Even some of my closest friends told me I was a fool to ditch my career to pursue deep-seeded passions that were still a bit fuzzy to me.

"What will you do for money?" one friend asked me.

"Write," I said. "I've always wanted to write. I freelance for a business magazine now. I'll just focus on finding more clients."

"There's no money in freelance writing," she scoffed at me.

Her words hurt me. And not because they were true - they were *far* from true - but because I didn't have her support. At that very vulnerable time in my life, I felt desperate for her support. Sometimes changing your life requires you to move in the opposite direction of those around you. Good friends will caution you with love. Great friends will root for you, even if you don't take their advice.

With all of this uncertainly swirling around me, I decided I needed to talk to a counselor. I had seen one several months prior for hypnosis in an effort to quit smoking. Now I found myself reaching out to her on a psychological level. Going back to see Kelley was just what I needed, and not because she was a licensed counselor with a cozy chair and a box of tissues next to it. She could relate to exactly what I was going through. I mean, *exactly*. Listening to someone else tell me they struggled with the same questions put me at ease. I believe I was led back to her so I could see I wasn't alone in this struggle. I was just one in a million who felt this way. And the fact that I wanted change was okay. Truth be told, it made me feel a *hell* of a lot better knowing I *wasn't* alone.

Kelley told me that once upon a time she had been a substance abuse councilor, working a mundane 9 to 5 job that eventually burned her out. After years of doing the same thing without growth, she realized she needed change. She felt no joy, no satisfaction. She was grateful for her job, just like me, but that gratefulness simply couldn't match the disdain she felt.

"In a very Buddha kind of moment," she told me, "I decided I wanted to leave my job and learn hypnotherapy. I had never done it before, but I was pretty sure I wanted to do it. I had to give up a lot to make the change. I was lucky enough to have a supportive husband, too. But with or without him, I would have done it. I would have found a way. So I left my job and went back to school."

"Just like that?" I asked with big eyes.

"Well, no. Not just like that. It was weeks of worry and wonder and decision-making. But I knew I was doing the right thing. I always knew."

"And are you happy now?" I asked her.

"Yeah! Oh, yeah. I love what I do."

"That's how I want to feel," I said. "I just don't know how to get there. I know I want to write, that's for sure. But I want to help people, too. I want to help people that are as unhappy as I am and guide them to a better place. I'm just not sure *how*. I need to figure it out before I explode."

"Is Mark supportive?" she asked me.

"Incredibly. He's the entire reason I came back to talk to you," I assured her. "He's very supportive."

"That's often half the battle, you know, finding someone that will support your decisions. Does Mark believe you can both handle the cost of living if you decide to leave your job?"

"Funny you should ask that," I said, leaning back in the cozy chair. "He seems to think we can."

"Well, figure it out," she suggested. "I bet it's entirely possible. Don't tell yourself it's not. Anything is possible when you put your mind to it."

I left Kelley's office that morning full of new hope. I drove home envisioning myself as a writer. More than that, I began to see myself as a motivational figure, on a stage in front of hundreds of people, sharing a truly heartfelt message that would lead them on a path that would change their view of life and love forever.

Later that night Mark and I huddled at our desk in the office and talked. We played with numbers and scratched our heads, trying to figure out how we could afford our now-merged life in light of this intense, indescribable transformation I was experiencing. None of which, by the way, felt wrong. That's the amazing part. My mind and body were telling me that leaving my job was absolutely the right thing to do. My father thought I was nuts.

"You want to do *what?*" he said when I told him, his mouth full of peanuts.

"I'm not happy, Dad. I don't really like my job."

"How can you not like your job? Look how far you've come!" he bellowed, bits of chewed peanut falling from his mouth.

"I know. But I just don't enjoy it anymore. I can't live my life doing something I don't enjoy."

"Yes you can. People do it every day. I did." He shoved another handful of nuts into his mouth.

I didn't pursue the subject any further. If he didn't get it now, he was never going to. But Mark got it. And if I haven't said it yet, I 'll say it now; I am *so* grateful for his support. He didn't question me once about taking the leap. As a matter of fact, I was shocked when he agreed that I needed to move on. There was no argument and no question. It was like he could read my heart. I wish for everybody looking to make passion-based change to have the same kind of support I have, yet I know that's not always possible. More often than not, the people closest to you will discourage you before *encouraging* you because they don't want to see you succeed. Usually it's because they want to make change too, only they don't have the courage they now sense in you to do so. But there are people out there that will cheer you on when you break the news that you intend to change jobs or move out of state or marry someone they've never met. There are people that will guide you to the right place when you announce that you intend on having a baby all on your own or that you're leaving your job as a defense attorney to become a missionary in South Africa. I promise you, *they are out there.* And once you become clear and open to what it is you want to change, despite any kind of resistance, the floodgates will open and the right people will appear. They're out there. Maybe not in the traditional form of father, mother, sibling, husband, wife, friend or co-worker, but I promise you, they are out there.

After about four weeks of soul-searching and contemplation, I was pretty sure I had a handle on what I believed I should be doing with my life, but some corners of it were still fuzzy. I continued to see Kelley, talk to Mark, cry my eyes out and read every self-development book I could get my hands on in an effort to find my life purpose. After four intense weeks of journaling and undergoing what I would describe as a transformational and amazing awakening, I finally realized what I was meant to do. Actually, I've always known. I just buried it under layers of alcohol, depression, disbelief and self-loathing. I buried it so far down that when it finally surfaced I burst open with so many emotions and feelings that I can't even begin to describe it. There was joy and relief and extreme happiness mixed in with a little bit of fear and a lot of curiosity. It's what some would call pain-filled joy. And it all came pouring out of me at once. I laughed like a hyena and cried like a baby at the same time. It's a damn good thing I was home alone when it happened, otherwise Mark would have me locked up on a desolate island somewhere. If you're wondering what I was doing and where I was during this crucial moment in my exploration of self, I was sitting in the center of my bed reading Dan Millman's, *The Life You were Born to Live* when I discovered what it was I wanted to do with my life. And like I said – I've always known. It just wasn't *clear*. Sometimes it takes the words or actions of others to slap you into reality. Millman's book and his breakdown of numerology finally made it clear to me: I could help people and write by *teaching*. And not necessarily in the classroom, but on a spiritual level; a level where I could help others understand that there was only one way to live life – with abundant love and passion. Not only would I help them *understand* that, I would help them get there too.

So that was the good news, finally realizing what I truly wanted to do with my life. The not-so-good news was that it didn't come in the form of a 9 to 5 job that I could find in the "help wanted" section of my local newspaper. If I was going to pursue such a path, it had to be on my own. That meant leaving a job with a steady paycheck, a decent pension, free cable and health insurance behind me. Goodbye, company perks, goodbye, job security. In hindsight, however, none of that really mattered. What I was feeling inside began to excite me and fill me with an energy I had never felt before. For the first time in my life I felt alive; and I was *very* eager to follow the signs and the voice inside me that had been leading me to this very moment.

I did end up going back to work. On some level I was hoping the way I felt about my career choice would change once I walked through the doors, but it didn't. I didn't fall back in love with what I was doing. But I went everyday anyway. Why? Because I was independent. I had always been independent. And everyday I went back, I wondered when the moment would come for me to kick-start the change. After five months of the same emotional uncertainty, I just couldn't do it anymore. It was time. So I typed up my resignation in an email late one night, crying like a baby the entire time. I explained my need to leave and expressed my gratitude and appreciation to my employer at the same time. Despite my feelings, he needed to know I appreciated him on every level. It was just time for me to move on.

I sat there staring at my note for about twenty minutes before I hit send. But when I finally did, I felt so *relieved!* All of the months of contemplation and soul-searching and questioning and guilt melted away the second I hit send. *Just like that.* I had finally mustered up the courage to take the leap. What is it that Martin Luther King said?

"Faith is taking the first step even when you don't see the whole staircase."

In preparation for my ascent on an invisible staircase, I decided to take all of my retirement and pay off as many bills as I could. Thus began the quest of self-employment, which turned out to be the most fulfilling and rewarding journey I have ever been on. (Other than motherhood, of course.) I mustered up courage I never knew I had and left my job as a television reporter to follow a deep-seeded passion. I now realize that every person in this world, no matter who they are, how old they are, where they come from or what they've done in the past, *everyone* should inevitably follow their passions and desires on *every level*. Sometimes that means leaving a relationship that is toxic or starting a new one that brings joy. Other times it means going back to school at age 52 or packing up all of your things to drive across the country. It could mean traveling through Europe for a month or seeking out your birth parents. Whatever it is that you want to do, just *do it*. There simply is no other way to live. Dreams and desires were planted within us for a reason. They are not to be ignored or pushed aside. They must be nurtured and tended to. They simply must.

Imagine your passion or dream as a tiny seed. It starts out small, right? Usually with just a thought. But then it grows. When you give that seed plenty of love and attention, it flourishes into a beautiful flower. But some of us ignore our little seedling. We don't water it with love or feed it with drive. So it withers up and dies. Just like that. This is where you've got to turn things around by saying *yes* to your dreams, *yes* to your desires and *yes* to your potential. You have ability within you that you can't even begin to imagine; talents and skills that you haven't even begun to explore yet. And when they begin to surface, you're going to be amazed.

During a conference in Salt Lake City, Utah some years ago, world-renowned motivational speaker Les Brown shared these words with the audience from someone that inspired him:

> "The ideal situation for a man or woman to die is to have family members praying with them as they cross over. But imagine if you will, being on your deathbed and standing around your bed are the ghosts of the ideas, the dreams, the abilities and the talents given to you by life. And you, for whatever reason, never acted on them. You never pursued that dream or used those talents. We never saw your leadership. You never used your voice or wrote that book. And there they all are, standing around your bed looking at you with large, angry eyes saying, "*We* came to you! And only *you* could have given us life. But now we must die with you." The question is: if you die today, what ideas, what dreams, what abilities, what talents, what gifts – will die with you?"

I don't want it to be this way. Not for me. I don't want to leave this earth aching because I didn't follow my heart or listen to my gut as it screamed at me day in and day out. I want to live. I want to have adventure. And I know damn well you do, too.

Chapter 2:

There is no such thing as instant gratification.

"Every successful journey, regardless of how long or difficult, begins with a simple step that is animated by gumption, directed by goals and repeated so often as necessary by dogged perseverance." - Thomas Campbell

While on a mini-vacation to Canada to see the Boston Red Sox play the Toronto Blue Jays, we made a point to spend a full day wandering around the Toronto zoo so that Maddie-Mae, my sweet and spunky 7-year-old, could finally see a real snow leopard. Mark drove and Maddie sang a made-up zoo song in the back seat, her little feet and hands moving to the rhythm of her tune. I watched the cars zip past me on the highway not really thinking about anything in particular when a white SUV caught my attention. Painted on the side window in big red and black letters read: *Lose up to 10 pounds in 20 minutes!! Call now!!*

"Where's my cell phone?" I asked out loud, searching the contents of the car next to my armrest.

"Who are you calling?" Mark asked me.

"That number on that truck right there. See it? It says I can lose up to ten pounds in twenty minutes. That's not true!" I was miffed as I watched the SUV zip through traffic and out of sight.

Mark patted my knee with a grin, knowing full well I wasn't going to call anybody.

"There are people out there that actually believe things like that," I said. "Life doesn't work that way."

And it doesn't.

I imagine the sign was for one of those places that wrap you up, shove you in a steam room and soak every ounce of water out of your body. Yes, you lose water weight, only to gain it back within a day. I've heard of brides doing such a thing the morning of their wedding. And if that's their prerogative, that's fine. But somebody out there isn't going to know that's how it works and will walk into it with higher expectations, only to feel defeated and disappointed when they learn it's not really a short cut to becoming a size two. Bottom line, there are no short cuts. Sure, we can cut across a field to get home from school or the store and call *that* a short cut, but as far as creating a perfection we think will make us happy:

a)   there is no quick fix.

b)   how unfortunate some of us believe there is.

In the quest for perfection there is a path that some will follow because they are told they will find instant gratification. It's plastered on billboards, laid out glamorously between the pages of magazines and spouted by highly paid actors and actresses on late night info-mercials. Even online dating sites promise instant love in six months or your money back. I've bought into these miraculous life-changing ideals dozens and dozens of times. By the time I was 14, I had a dresser drawer full of diet pills that vowed could make me thinner than I could possibly imagine - in just two weeks. I remember my father discovering the pills and accusing me of using them as speed, which I can honestly say I never considered. Then there was the GH System. Ask my dear friend Jennifer about that one. As sprouting young women in the 8th grade, we longed for fairy tale love with the perfect man. But where would we find him? The answer came to us in the back of a tabloid magazine. For only $19.99, we could get the GH System (GH standing affectionately for "Get Him") and all of our problems would be solved. I don't remember what the contents of the system were when we finally received it, but I can tell you neither one of us found the perfect man (or boy, as they were at that time) in the 8th grade.

It's no secret that mainstream media and expert marketing gurus have discovered the best way to sell their product is to promise "instant results". Got wrinkles? Buy some magic lotion. Want to lose weight? Take a pill, eat a cookie that puffs up in your tummy or shake a salt-like substance on your food to kill your appetite. It simply doesn't work that way. There is no such thing as instant gratification. No pill or spray or salt-like shaker is going to make you thin in two weeks or less. But there is good news. There is a power within you, an ancient power, that when tapped, will not only astound and amaze you - it will show you a rather simple and abundant-filled life that can make *anything* possible. Hundreds of thousands of people are rediscovering it and their lives are changing. These people are opening their minds to the realm of possibility where compassion and love exist; to a place where you have the power and ability to mold your life just the way you want it. In this place, you learn to love yourself and that is really the key. Once you learn to love who you are, miracles will happen. None of us is perfect, yet we strive for perfection anyway. We see imperfection as we measure ourselves against the airbrushed models who are stick thin and likely haven't eaten in a week. And that's not a criticism. It's a reality that is killing thousands of people everyday - physically, mentally and spiritually.

The ads and billboards I refer to aren't just selling a product, they're selling *concepts* of perfect love, perfect bodies and perfect lives. They're telling us that how we look is more important than anything else. So we work to fit the mold. And when we don't fit the mold we're made to feel ashamed and guilty. What's missing in all of this is reality. Because we're so programmed to accept these visuals as reality, we become confused and frustrated when we don't get what we want in five seconds or less. Whatever change you want to make, *it will happen.* You will succeed. It just takes time. It doesn't matter who you are, where you come from, where you live, what you've done in the past, how old you are or how much money you say you have or don't have, if there is a hunger within you and a passion to go with it, then you own the ability to have, do or be anything you want.

When I got my first job as a television reporter I was thrilled beyond the definition of the word. Why wouldn't I be? All of the egos that mocked me in junior high and high school would see that I was worthy of recognition. They would see that I was an important figure in society, responsible for bringing them the most updated information in their community. Then they would look at me and think, *"Wow. She must be really smart, landing a job as a reporter and all!"* I know now that this isn't what it's all about, but in growing I thought status mattered. So when I got my first job, I was more than ready to accept my assignments with no questions and bring the public their answers in a timely fashion, ready to go live at 6 o'clock with bells on.

For starters I sucked at going live. I desperately wanted to be good at it, but let's face it, I just wasn't. I sounded like one of those people that *tries* to sound intelligent, but doesn't, and everyone knows that they aren't intelligent. You know the kind? Yeah. That was me. And my hair looked better than my on-air delivery, for goodness sake. I also couldn't conduct an interview to save my life. I didn't know what to ask and most of the time I didn't even know what the hell I was talking about anyway. My first city council meeting brought me to my knees. I probably should have paid more attention during "Participation in Government" in high school because I was completely lost the first time I sat down to listen to the decision makers in Watertown, New York. I remember going back to the station and the senior reporter asking me questions that I simply couldn't answer.

"So what did they talk about?" he asked me.

"I have no idea."

He laughed as he buzzed about the newsroom, getting ready for the 11 o'clock newscast. "No, seriously. Did they talk about the salt pile? Or the PILOT program? They were supposed to vote on the PILOT program for the city."

I didn't want to answer him because I didn't know. I tried to stay focused in the meeting, but I couldn't. Lawmakers were voting yay or nay and I didn't keep count because I was so busy stressing about what the hell a PILOT program was.

"I guess I have to go back and listen to the tape," I said, ducking into an edit bay. He stood there staring at me through the edit bay window for a moment, and then walked away.

It didn't take long before I realized being a television reporter was *a lot* of work. I didn't get to just shove a microphone under someone's nose and say, *"What*

do you think of the latest trend in clothes?" There was
government and politics and I didn't like any of it. What's
more, if I didn't know about a particular topic, I had to
research it and I wanted no part of that. I just wanted
to go out, get the story in ten minutes or less and come
back to the station and edit it. Forget the details. Who
cares? Just about every day, a simple story like milk
prices going up would turn into a whole big thing where
I had to interview not just one farmer to get his reaction
on the situation, I had to interview *three*. And then I had
to call their congressman, find out how long milk prices
fluctuated and why, and then drive around the North
Country shooting video of farms and cows and milk
cartons and little kids drinking out of the milk cartons
until the cows came home. And *then*...I would have
to go back to the station to write the story (finishing
it at 5:20, which would leave me less than 20 minutes
to edit) and my news director would ask me, "Did you
call Farmer Ed from the Dell to find out what *he's* doing
about this?"

And of course I didn't.

This vicious cycle went on for almost a year. I
would get my assignment every morning and pray it
wouldn't require more than posing questions to people
on the street. If I did end up with what I considered a
"complicated" story, I would get creative and try to write
it avoiding the primary issue altogether. That never really
worked, however. My news director would call me over
to his desk and ask, "Did you look into what they're
doing about this right now?"

I finally had to admit to myself that there were no
shortcuts, ultimately recognizing that my job took work.
A *lot* of it. If I wanted to put out a decent story I had to
put the necessary time and energy into it. That meant
when the guy I was interviewing told me his house was

built on a Brownfield site, I had to be brave enough to ask him what that was (if I didn't already know) and then further educate myself on the subject via research when I got back to the station. Reporters don't know everything, despite the general public's expectation that they should. They have to read and study and ask questions about new topics everyday. That's how they learn. Putting a decent news story together takes time. Getting everything right takes time. And so does making change.

I'm going to get a little personal here and talk about some things in my life that I'm not proud of. I choose to do this to show you how long I've been working to bring myself to a safe and beautiful place in my life. Many of my friends and family don't even know about these things. I call these things demons, and I do so because they've haunted me for years, choking me and mocking me and threatening to suck the very life out of me. When I tried to shoo them away they always found their way back, only to laugh at me as I weakly opened the door to let them in. My demons hounded me in the form of addiction. And there are times they are still very brutal.

The first one that devoured any self-love I had for myself came in the form of an eating disorder. I was 13-years-old when it began. I'm 39 as I write this, and I still struggle with the emotional turmoil of it all. I'm also writhing in my seat as I type this because it's uncomfortable to think about. I've been fighting a battle with this demon for 26 years. *Twenty-six years.* I hate even talking about it because for those that don't understand it, the act of what people put themselves through in an effort to stay thin is considered disgraceful and wholly without purpose. In this I have learned not to judge anyone with any addiction of any kind, including food, alcohol, drugs, sex, gambling, caffeine, reality TV shows, soap operas, eating chalk, *whatever.* They *all* exist. Addiction is very real. Alcoholism and drug use are still the most prevalent addictions that people battle. I mention this because I suffered those demons, too. I have the trifecta of addictions and I've kept them hidden for years. I would put a smile on the outside, but suffered deeply on the inside. I didn't want anyone to know I had to rely on something else to make me feel better. I didn't want to get called out on my addictions, either. As comedian Mitch Hedberg once said, "Alcoholism is the only disease you can actually get in trouble for having." He overdosed on cocaine and heroin in a hotel room in New Jersey in 2005.

I created a timeline recently that shows when my addictions began and when I was able to get them under control. None of them were short-lived, nor did I kick them out of my life overnight. No pill, spray or salt helped me shoo them away, either. It took falling down, getting up and falling down again and again and again and a *hundred more* agains before I became *so* exhausted with the struggle, I had no choice but to stop. And even that was a challenge. So here it is:

- Eating Disorder: 1985 – 2011 (26 YEARS)
- Smoking: 1985 – 2009 (24 YEARS)
- Binge Drinking: 2000 – 2009 (8 YEARS)
- Drug Use: 1985 – 2009 (24 YEARS)

The first time I did the math I was stunned. I just stood there looking at the numbers and cried. Twenty-six years? I've had an eating disorder for twenty-six years? And drug use? Really? I dabbled with marijuana for *twenty-four years?* There were many periods during that time I didn't touch the stuff. I would go months, sometimes years without smoking it, let alone even thinking about it, but I always went back.

I also spent at least five years on an anti-depressant. Personally, I didn't enjoy that one bit. When I went to my doctor asking for a different, more holistic means of working through my depression, he didn't really entertain other options. Instead, he upped my dosage. I didn't want to take anymore, period. So in 2009, I weaned myself off of the drug, another task that wasn't easy. For the better part of a year, I experienced "brain tremors" and horrific dreams. My mood swings were terrible. I suffered these side effects for a long time, but I never gave up.

I put this timeline before you to show you that it doesn't matter how long you've dealt with your demon(s), if you're looking to make change and move away from the darkness, it absolutely can be done. Yes, it's going to take work. And yes, it's going to take time. But what have you got to lose? The wonderful thing about this intention of yours is that you *don't* have to look outside your door or in a secret location for the power and strength to change. It is already within you. And it always has been.

Chapter 3:

Change your thoughts, change your world.

"Your place in life is not fixed by heredity. You are not condemned by the lower levels of circumstance or lack of opportunity." – Wallace Wattles

"Few appreciate the real power of the mind, and no one remains fully aware of it all the time." – A Course In Miracles

The power and strength I speak of doesn't require a Ouija board or magic potion to access it (although some Shamans have been known to use psychedelic drugs to release mental and cultural ideals, allowing them to see their true nature, free from cultural programming). The idea is to tap into that wisdom purely and wholly, understanding all the while that you can live a life of free will where you can have, do or be anything you want. You have so much more control over you life than you realize. You can regain that control by using one simple concept that has been used for thousands and thousands of years: regulating your thoughts.

If it sounds too good to be true, that's because we as Westerners have lost the ability to live our own lives and make our own decisions *because* of cultural programming. If our father was a drunk, so we will be too. If our mother was depressed and our grandmother was depressed, so we will be too. If our family lived in poverty, so we will live too, and so on. Most of us live fairly unconsciously in this way, thinking that life is a dark entity purposely happening *to* us - and we are a victim. The bottom line is that if we choose to believe these kinds of thoughts and continue to think along these lines, *nothing will ever change.* The negative web we weave is a tangle of limiting beliefs – and the way we think is directly influencing what is happening in our lives. If we are willing to change the way we think, amazing and eye-opening possibilities will begin to reveal themselves and our lives will move in a completely different direction. This effect, otherwise known as the Law of Attraction, has been the subject of strength and prosperity with New Thought authors like Wallace D. Waddles and Napoleon Hill since the late 19th and early 20th century.

The Law of Attraction is a long-standing metaphysical belief that positive thoughts bring about positive results and negative thoughts bring about negative results. According to the New Thought authors that have studied and practiced the Law of Attraction, statements like "I have no money" actually keep us in the realm of *having no money.* To turn this around, we need to change the focus of our thoughts to produce the opposite attraction. Therefore, instead of focusing on what you *don't* have, change the thought to leave your head as if what you seek is already in your possession. "I have great wealth and more than enough money" or, "I have a job that I love with a six figure income."

Basically, the thoughts you put out into the universe, good or bad, will undoubtedly come back to you again and again. In line with this, as you continue to create negative thoughts and feelings within you, you ultimately lose sight of your *actual* reality, which may be completely free of negativity at that very moment where you revel in negativity. Allow me to pose an example:

You're sitting at your desk in an office with several other people. Everyone is working away, minding their own business and keeping to themselves. You look up toward the back of the office where "Amy" sits. Just three days before, you felt she insulted and embarrassed you in front of your coworkers. You didn't say anything at the time. Instead you went home, told your spouse what happened, and have been living the moment over and over again in your mind ever since; only this time you've added the perfect comeback which includes applause from your coworkers as they carry you around victoriously on their shoulders. Despite the contrived victory you've added, you still continue to live with the pain of what happened three days prior. And now you've blown it up into a feature length film where Renee Zellweger plays Amy, and the beautiful and effervescent Angelina Jolie portrays you, the star of your film.

Now here's the reality of the situation: at that very moment when you are sitting quietly at your desk, *nothing is wrong*. No one is even talking to you. The entire office, Amy included, is busy. You, however, have stepped *out* of the present moment and into the *past* to pull up the weeds of that painful moment. If you smacked yourself on the forehead and pulled yourself back to the present moment you would see that there actually is no pain or hurt. Amy's words were taken out with the garbage three days before. Quite frankly, it's very possible no one even remembers the event from three days ago. But you let your thoughts take off anyway. You single-handedly created your own suffering - and *this* is where you need to turn things around in order to make change.

A brilliant man by the name of Eckhart Tolle recognized this change in consciousness after spending years of suffering in negative, unproductive thought. In a fleeting moment of "no thought", as he calls it, he recognized a sense of peace and stillness: a place of pure bliss where nothing was wrong. Tolle says that 98% of the suffering we feel is inflicted *not* by the "Amy's" of the world, but by *ourselves*. What's more, instead of living in the present moment (at your desk where it's quiet and still and no one is insulting you), we tend live in the past (where the insult happened) or in the future (where Amy gets fired or hit by a truck) - where we think life is better and *far* more important than the moment we're in right *now*.

Tolle's philosophies on thought are nothing new. They come from the wisdom of Christian, Buddhist, Zen and Taoist teachings, all of which go back hundreds and hundreds of years. But somewhere along the line, we lost sight of how to live freely. We let those around us tell us what we can and cannot do; and for some, the results have been devastating. All it takes to make change is the will to want, the commitment to do it and the desire to really, really be free.

During some very trying times in my life I fought like hell, each and every time, to pull myself out of the abyss of pain I constantly found myself in. I knew deep down in my soul there was an answer to my freedom and happiness; I just didn't know where to find it. During one of these times, I remember sitting in the airport with my family, waiting for a delayed plane that would eventually take us to Disney World. It was a trip graciously financed by my father for my then 5-year-old daughter. I needed something – *anything* – to help me change my thoughts from gloom and doom to sunshine and butterflies. I took my daughter's hand and we walked through the airport to an overpriced bookstore where dozens of travelers mulled the shelves to pass the time. While Maddie marveled at the Barbie book I put in her hands, I scanned a tiny self-help section for an answer. As I stood there with my heart aching, I remembered how I would do the very same thing in the years after I graduated college. I was so, so lost in those days. And for some reason, I thought I could find the answer on a shelf in Wal-Mart or K-Mart. It sounds odd, but I would literally walk up and down every aisle until something that came in a box or plastic container jumped out at me and said, *Here! Over here! Buy me and all of your pain and suffering will go away!* I was too naive to realize I was looking for instant gratification; a quick fix to remove the pain and replace it with bliss and contentment. This time I was looking for wise words from another aching soul that could help me get back on track.

"What is your book, Mommy?" Maddie was looking up at me with a beautiful little smile.

"Oh, it's just a book about – making things better." I was holding a copy of Lisa Nichols' *No Matter What!* in my hands.

"What do you need to make better? Ways to make you stop crying?"

Her statement stunned me. She had seen my cry so many times but never said anything before. And there were plenty of times when she would stroke my hair telling me it was okay, "uh-cuz the next day will be better, Mommy."

I realized at that moment that I really, really needed to make change or my negative and self-destructive behaviors were going to destroy not only me, but her little soul as well. And I didn't want that. No way. Children are so naive, living in an innocuous and perfect world – a world that many of us don't remember; a world where God keeps us innocent and pure with a beautiful, white light that shields us from the pain and suffering of a vicious, harmful outer-world. And then, inevitably, something happens that pulls us out of that perfectness. That's when the struggle begins.

"Do I cry a lot?" I asked her with a forced smile.

"Yes. But it's okay, Mommy. I cry sometimes, too."

I bought the book (and the Barbie one, too) and spent the entire vacation reading it and taking notes (save the time I was running around Disney with my child). After a full day at the park I would get her ready for bed, read her a story, kiss her on the forehead and then crawl under the blankets next to her to delve into my own book. I wanted knowledge; as much as I could get my hands on so that I could pull myself out of the darkness and start living a healthier, more productive and passionate life. Much of what I was reading was common sense. But let's face it - in the wallows of pity, common sense is the furthest thing from our minds. Of all the elements I took from the book, one in particular stuck with me and I still use it today. I imagine an invisible stop button on my forehead. When I start moving backward into the past and reliving painful events, I do what Nichols suggests: I pretend there's a stop button on my forehead and I physically reach up and push it to "stop" the negative thoughts from rolling. I imagine anyone standing around me when I'm doing this thinks I either have a minor scratch on my forehead or I don't know how to scratch at all. But no matter.

Whatever it took to change my way of thinking, I was willing to do it. I still use this little exercise to this day.

Motivational author and self-help pioneer Louise Hay uses positive affirmations to turn negative beliefs into optimistic, prosperous ones. Here is one from a set of affirmation cards she created for people like you and me:

"I am willing to release my old patterns and negative beliefs. The power that created me has given me the power to create my new life. I choose positive, fulfilling new thoughts. I begin anew – right here, right now."

Write that down on an index card and tape it up somewhere in your bathroom or bedroom. You know, I just said I took one thing in particular from Nichols' book, but that's not true. This was a practice she did too. She encouraged her readers to write down positive statements and put them everywhere in their homes. I still do this. As a matter of fact, when I first started dating Mark, I remember buzzing around my house to make sure it was in perfect order, intending to remove my little affirmations so that he wouldn't think he was dating a kook. (Kook is my definition of a nut job with serious issues.) I yanked some of them down, but not all of them. And when I realized he was standing in my kitchen reading one that said, *I am a good woman and an even better mother. I am on my way to greater things,* I almost died.

"I – I need to remind myself of the good things," I stammered as I reached for the index card.

"Don't take it down," he said stopping me. "I like them."

"Really? You do? You don't think I'm crazy?"

He smiled at me gently and pulled a business card out of his wallet. He turned it over and held it in front of my face. On the back was written:

I live in the now. Each moment is new. I choose to see my self-worth. I love and approve of myself.

Like me, he was using positive affirmations to rewire his brain and think in a completely different way than he had before. Right now, even as I clickity-clack on my keyboard, that business card is on the side of our refrigerator for both of us to see everyday. The more you think good, the more good you receive. It's the Law of Attraction and it's working in you and around you, whether you choose to believe it or not.

If you're thinking positive affirmations are phooey, I can understand why you would think so. At first the concept sounds like it requires some sort of magic or hocus-pocus, and we all know that stuff is reserved for the Princesses at Disneyland. For some of us it's a foreign concept. How can repeating something over and over again bring us what we want? Because that's the power of the universe and that's just how it works. It's been scientifically proven over and over again.

One such experiment took place in Geneva, Switzerland, in 1997. Dr. Nichoas Gisin of the University of Geneva conducted an experiment with the help of his colleagues to show that there are always energetic connections between "things", regardless of where those "things" are in our world.

Basically, Gisin took one particle of matter and split it into two, sending one half seven miles north and the other seven miles south along optical telephone fibers. The results were uncanny. Although he had *physically* split the particle in half, the particles were still connected *energetically*. We can try to visualize this by imagining two tiny little balls hovering in the air, equal distance apart. Now imagine a white, wavering line of "energy" coming out of each ball and meeting in the middle. The balls, or particles, are indeed in two different places, but an invisible energy, the white, wavering line, still keeps them together. To further show that the particles were still related, Gisin intentionally disturbed or "shook" the particle in the north. The result was that the particle's distant twin experienced the exact same "shaking" at the same moment, despite the fact there was no physical link. This tells us that we don't have to physically be a part of someone or something to still be connected to it. Scientist and visionary Gregg Braden says we were all once part of the same little particle that created the universe today, which means we are all still very much linked.

"We've been taught that we are separate from the world," Braden said during an interview for Louise Hay's movie, *You Can Heal Your Life*. "Now technology has come so far that our very existence is threatened by the technology that we've developed. To survive we have to write ourselves back into the equation with our prayers, our beliefs and our affirmations. When spoken through the language of the heart, these affirmations have a direct, powerful and immediate impact on our bodies and the world around us. This phenomenon invites us to become very aware of what we hold true in our hearts. What we think is what we become.

"What we're beginning to understand is that human emotion and feeling and belief is a *language*, a non-verbal language that the universe recognizes and understands," he continued. "It doesn't know real time. This is why the key is to be very specific about what we choose to bring into our lives, because what we're doing in the world of quantum possibilities is isolating and locking what we want into place. If were not specific then how can the universe be specific about what it gives to us?"

Thus, what you think, you become. You create. You manifest.

When I left television to pursue writing and speaking, I had to take action to find work. I scoured the newspapers and put my feelers out. I also affirmed out loud, every day, that work would come to me. I would say (and still say), *I am a very much sought after speaker and writer. People call me, email me or reach out to me via social networking looking to hire me. They pay me very well for one hour of my time. I fly first class and stay in the finest hotels and resorts and sometimes I get free spa visits. I love what I do and I do what I love.*

I would say this everyday. And then I would wait. Sometimes I would get frustrated because days would go by and nothing would manifest. Admittedly, I would get mad at myself for affirming things that weren't happening. I didn't realize I was looking for *instant gratification*. Remember, the universe doesn't know about time; it just aligns its energies to bring you what you ask for. Sometimes it takes days, sometimes weeks or even months, but it always happens. Always. Add a few bonuses in your affirmation, too. That's what I did with the spa visits! They have nothing to do with speaking, but there's nothing like a good massage or pedicure from time to time.

Just a few weeks after I left news in 2010, Mark and I decided we wanted to get married. We were giddy about our decision and began planning a wedding right away. I wanted to get married in the fall and we both wanted a small, simple wedding with family only. When we realized we didn't require much we decided to pull it off and get married on October 30th, 2010. That gave us eight weeks to plan. During the planning process, a friend of Marks kindly put together an impromptu engagement shin-dig at a premiere bar and restaurant in Syracuse. Dozens of people came, including attorneys from the Onondaga County District Attorney's office where Mark had worked as a prosecutor for over a decade. So there I was, chatting away with friends when a man that was very familiar to me approached me. We started chatting about news and all the fun conversation that goes with it when it hit me who he was - Dave White, the communications director for the school of Environmental Science and Forestry in Syracuse. He was someone I had spoken with a hundred times during my time as a reporter, but I hadn't recognized him outside of the college with a cold beer in his hand. I also didn't know he was married to an assistant district attorney, thus the reason he was at the engagement shin-dig. When I told him I had just left the news business and was working as a freelance writer, he immediately pulled out his business card and said, "Call me. I think I may have some work for you."

Well, I called him. And today SUNY-ESF is one of my best and most lucrative clients. Not only do I cover and write about local events or milestones at the college, I also write and edit the video for a weekly environmental segment that airs, quite ironically, on the very television station that I left to pursue my passions.

The same week the ESF opportunity manifested, something else came my way. I was leaving a bookstore when my phone signaled I had email. I got into my car and proceeded to read it. It was from a woman at a vineyard in the Thousand Islands. She said she had gotten my name from the editor of a business magazine that I write for and she wanted to know if I would be interested in writing for them. I was stunned. So much so, I began to cry. And laugh. For the second time in a week, I had been contacted by a source that I had never reached out to in the first place. They came to me. Per my affirmation, *they came to me.* Interestingly enough, they came just as I was losing faith in the pull of the universe. It was like the cosmos were saying, *Be patient. We're working here. It will come.*

I have to say that the same thing happened regarding speaking engagements. I spent several days cold-calling businesses and organizations, offering my services as a speaker for free in an effort to get myself out there. I emailed, left voice mails and snail-mailed information to dozens of places throughout Central New York. Nothing. And then about a month or so later, I got an email. And then another. And then another! Again, the opportunities came just as I lost faith. This time the universe slapped me in the face and said, *There's no such thing as instant gratification! It will come. Trust, and it will come.*

Thanks to these two situations (and there are others, too), I do trust that it will come. And I have fun with it. That's the beauty of this whole thing. You never know how your desires will manifest before you. When it unfolds in a way that you never expected, revel in it. The more you play, the more you stay in the game. Will you lose faith? Oh, yes. Many times. But you'll learn from it and get right back up.

Chapter 4:

When you fall apart.

"The depth and strength of a human character are defined by its moral reserves. People reveal themselves completely only when they are thrown out of the customary conditions of their life, for only then do they have to fall back on their reserves." – Leonardo da Vinci

I had a really bad day one Monday. I woke up tired, showered tired and sat down at my computer tired. It was grey and rainy outside. I was on the edge of a cold that gripped me for the better part of a week and I didn't sleep well because of it. I also didn't sleep well because I couldn't shut my mind off at night. I was thinking about my writing and my speaking and a book I was reading and religion and God and the winter solstice of 2012. I felt my editor didn't want to pay me fairly for a recent project and I wasn't sure how to handle the news of the day that Osama Bin Laden had been captured and killed. I eventually hit overload and before I realized it, I had "overcooked" and exploded into a blubbering, whiney, exhausted mess. Every affirmation and positive thought dissolved right before my eyes, and any affirmations that tried to stay with me met their demise when I shoved them out the door into the icy rain or set them on fire with a vanilla frosting scented candle. I'd had it.

Losing my faith only made me cry more. Just two days before I was happily skipping through daisy-filled fields in my mind, armed with every tool imaginable to conquer the demons and beasts that threatened to overpower me. I was invincible! Now my toolbox lay tipped over and empty at my feet. And man, was I *pissed* about it. Our big black lab was also at my feet, crushing my toes as he looked up at me silently.

The news of Bin Laden started the ball rolling. It was 5 a.m. when Mark nudged me awake to ask if I'd seen the news online yet. I don't have a computer behind my eyes so I'm not really sure why he was asking me that but I humored him anyway. I told him no and asked him why? He had to repeat himself at least three times because I couldn't understand him. That's not his fault, either. I wear earplugs at night. At first I thought he was talking about President Obama. But he was saying *Osama.*

"They got him. Shot him in the head," he told me.

I lay silently beside him with my arm over his torso as he scrolled through the news story on his Blackberry. And instead of jumping for joy or high-fiving my husband, I wondered what kind of retaliation this would bring. I also imagined all of the people I knew on Facebook who slammed the integrity of the President regularly would likely have a different opinion of him now. But more than that, more than either of these thoughts, was the idea that remarkable world events were happening closer and closer together; an idea researched and noted by several scientists and theologians that believe an ancient timeline designed by the Mayan civilization shows the end of a world age (*not* the end of the world), coming to a close on December 21st, 2012. And yes I do believe they are accurate and that this world age has been churning for the past two decades, but that's a conversation for another time.

Add to that the fact that I was bothered by a conversation with a friend where I felt he criticized me because I wouldn't call myself a Christian. That conversation was still very much alive in my head.

"How can you not be Christian? Don't you believe in God?" he scoffed.

"Yes, I do. I do believe in God. I believe in a powerful, all-knowing energetic entity that loves us all."

He stared at me blankly. "But you don't believe Jesus existed."

"Actually I do. I recently read a fantastic book about the history of that time and it's talks about the Dead Sea scrolls and the Gnostic gospels. So, I do believe he existed, but – "

" – but as a prophet," he said quickly, cutting me off.

"Yes," I said as gently as possible.

He scoffed at me again and shook his head.

I realize Christianity is the most practiced religion in the United States but I don't practice it. I have been in deep-faith circles with friends and even had the honor of speaking at an incredible Christian women's conference where I was surrounded by hundreds of women singing and crying out His name as they were moved by the Holy Spirit. I cried with them, feeling their joy and loving every second of it. On the other end of the spectrum, I spent several weeks at a Buddhist temple on the edge of the Pennsylvania-New York State line where I learned how to be at peace with myself and meditate. There, I fell in love with the concept of Buddha nature and the peaceful, loving path Buddhists follow as they work to achieve enlightenment. For me, experiencing and reading about the faith of others has helped me better understand the idea behind religion while falling more in line with a life of free-will. I have no steady religious practice, nor do I criticize or call into question the faith of others. But I was quickly learning that some people do, and I felt I was experiencing that criticism on a very personal level.

I sat completely agitated at my dining room table with all of these uncomfortable thoughts. With my laptop in front of me and a cup of tea beside me, I began to update my spreadsheets to bill clients, including the editor who I felt was fighting me on what I thought I should be paid for a recent project. The dog continued to step on my feet as the editor and I shot emails back and forth. My tea tasted horrible. Every thing I read was laced with Osama and I couldn't get the faith-based conversation with my friend out of my mind. I also couldn't stop coughing and my temperature was rising as absolute exhaustion set in. All of this was extremely bad timing for my very gentle and loving husband, who called during the break of a trial to see how I was.

"Do you want me to call your editor and talk to him?" he asked me.

"*What??* Call and *talk* to him? What, am I four?? Are you serious? Oh my GOD. I can't handle this. I gotta – I gotta hang up. I'm hanging up now."

And so I hung up. And then I cried. *Nothing* was going right. I felt I had destroyed my relationship with my Christian friend and lost one of my best-paying clients, which didn't matter anyway, because I was pretty sure my husband was about to file for divorce anyway. But not before the dog crushed my feet and the entire world blew up. I flopped myself in our papasan chair and wrapped a blanket around me.

Then a text came across my phone. It was Mark: *Please call me back.*

Oh, he was so good, so patient with me.

"I really shouldn't be talking to anyone right now," I said when I called him back. Tears were pouring down my cheeks. "I'm a horrible person!"

"No, you're not," he said gently.

"Well then I'm selfish. You're in trial and that is important and I'm not helping by sniveling over here about stupidness."

"It's not stupidness," he reminded me. "It's the day. You're just having a bad day. You're allowed to have a bad day once in a while, you know."

"What if he never talks to me again?" I asked, wiping the snot from my nose. I was referring to my friend. Sydney-dog was no longer on my feet. Now he was *at* my feet, staring up at me with his big, beautiful brown eyes. He wagged his tail gently with worry.

"Let me ask you this," Mark said. "Do you know for a fact he's angry with you?"

"Well, no. But it certainly sounded that way. He hasn't emailed me or sent me a message on Facebook since."

"That doesn't mean he's mad at you, honey. Maybe something else came up. Maybe in his family, you know? And maybe he's not near a computer right now."

"Everyone is near a computer right now!" I whined. "When haven't you seen someone *not* near a computer in the world of smartphones? Hell, my editor is near a computer right now! We've been curtly emailing each other for the past hour and a half!"

"Slow down," he said to me. "Just – slow – down."

"And the mainstream media isn't paying a bit of attention to the winter solstice of 2012. Is it all hooey? Am I crazy? I don't feel good. I need a nap. Where's our bed?"

"Stop," he said quietly. "Slow down."

Mark should either be a counselor or read children's books for a living because he has the most gentle and soothing voice I have ever heard, next to Mr. Rogers, of course. Instead, he's a criminal prosecutor, which I think makes his authenticity even more endearing. He's very real. He was also very right. I needed to slow down. I was creating scenarios and movies in my mind that were not actual realities. I had single-handedly created pain in my heart by thinking I was losing a friend, losing a writing gig, and losing my feet because Sydney-dog is a big, black lab. I realized all of this when Mark said something that I already knew; something I've read in dozens of books and lectured to others, including myself:

"Our worst demons are often the thoughts and scenarios we create in our heads. They don't actually exist. And in a moment of weakness, those damning thoughts can come tumbling back on us."

He was right. Isn't it funny how at that very moment, at that *very* vulnerable and highly sensitive moment, I *GOT* it? Sometimes that's all it takes, simply hearing the right words at the right time. Suddenly, the clouds lifted and the rain stopped. I peered over my blanket-covered lap where Sydney and my toolbox were waiting. The toolbox wasn't really empty. It was actually quite full. And now I had another tool to put in it: *change in perspective*. All day, I had viewed things negatively. I wrote and directed negative-minded movies while writing negative-sounding emails and sending negative affirmations out into the world. I had gotten so far into it, that all of the negative things began to layer atop one another and took me over completely. If I wanted to make it through the rest of the day, I needed to change my thoughts. And fast. I put my head back on the papasan and took a deep breath and said, "Everything is fine. Nothing is wrong at this moment. Absolutely nothing. Life is good and I am surrounded by goodness."

I allowed myself to decompress for several minutes. And when I did, the following happened:

1) I got an email from my friend telling me that he hoped I felt better soon and that he missed me. This made my blockbuster mind-movie where he wanted to end our friendship a complete bust. I sincerely doubt I'll make any money from this film now.

2) I sent my editor a more positive and appreciative e-mail, thanking him for his efforts to get me the maximum payment, which resulted in the same kind of email in return. This squelched the fear I placed in my head that I was going to "lose a client."

3) I remembered that there were still plenty of days left before December 21st, 2012, and that I needed to keep my promise to live each day to the fullest.

4) I kept my feet up for the rest of the day. By reclaiming my toes, I got my feet back and Sydney-dog was forced to lay on his own.

Every situation, whether it is negative and heart breaking or glorious and joyful, gives us a tool to use for experiences down the road. We don't recognize the gift in the moment, especially when it's a dark, negative moment. And why should we? In those moments we lose touch with what is really going on. We focus on everything that is going wrong, completely ignoring the things around us that are going right. In my moment, I had forgotten that I had a wonderful little girl and a very patient husband. I also had a roof over my head and a car in the driveway. I had my health and my talents and the ability to act on them. All of these things went out the window because I was so consumed with what I *didn't* have.

Another tool I gained that morning: *gratification*. The experiences I met with that day were necessary, laid out before me by the universe to help groom my path. They were unwelcome, no doubt, but absolutely necessary.

Life puts us exactly where we need to be at every given moment. Perhaps it's not a moment you're particularly fond of, but that's the deal. Sometimes it's at a job we don't really like or with people we don't necessarily care for. Every situation will leave us with a new tool to file away in our box. And than one day, seemingly out of nowhere, you'll pull that tool out. You'll smile a little too, as you remember the very situation you were in when you acquired it.

Many years ago I worked as a bartender at a chain restaurant in Syracuse. It was a decent job and it paid the bills. I knew it wasn't what I wanted to do for the rest of my life, but at the time it was what I had to do. I was on my own in a quaint, little apartment. I was proud of my new home, filled with unique pieces of furniture from a nearby flea market and my very generous parents. I loved my independence and knew I had to be responsible and work in order to maintain it. But believe me, there were days when I *just didn't want to go*. On one particularly sunny Saturday I got into my car begrudgingly, cursing the bartending gods for all of the thirsty patrons that would wander in that day. By the time I got to the first traffic light at the corner, I was miserable. The rest of the world was outside buzzing happily around on their bikes or in their yards running through rainbow colored sprinklers. I watched as one little girl in particular bounced happily through the water without a care in the world. I wanted to be that happy! I rolled my window down and shouted out to her with false glee, "Guess where I'm going, kid? I'm going to work!"

She stopped dead in the middle of the sprinkler and just stared at me. The stunned look on her face made me laugh.

"That's right, kid! I'm GOIN' TO WORK!"

And I zipped away in my car.

The mere thought of what I had done made me laugh even more. So I did it again. This time I stuck my head out the window and shouted to a duo on their bikes, "Woo-HOO! I'm goin' to work! YEAH! *Wooo!*"

I continued this nonsense all the way to the parking lot. And do you know what? By the time I walked in to the restaurant, I realized I didn't mind being there at all. I felt good! I had literally changed my perspective, which changed my thoughts, which brought me to a place that really wasn't so bad. I had gathered a new tool. I tell you this story because I picked up that tool almost fifteen years ago and I still use it today.

One step at a time, you will collect the tools necessary to complete your journey. If you seek a different line of work or career, every job you've had prior has given you a tool that you will inevitably use later in life. I used to maintain a musical instrument catalog both as a magazine and an online store. Eleven years later, I found I had retained much of what I learned and was able to build and manage my own website – down to troubleshooting it all by my big girl self. That was huge for me. I also learned in that same job how important it is to leave a detailed message on an answering machine.

"Talk slowly, give your purpose and say your phone number twice," my boss at the time told me. "You want them to know exactly who you are and give them a chance to write your phone number down."

I carried that with me into my career as a journalist and still do it to this day. I recently had to contact my doctor's office to let them know the date of a test I'd had. I left my name, the reason I called and my phone number, which I said twice, slowly. Then I thanked the answering machine and gave my name and phone number again. When the nurse called me back several hours later, she was tickled pink.

"I just want to thank you for leaving such a clear, concise message. If everyone would do that, it would make my life so much easier!"

As insignificant as an action or episode may seem, it carries a reason for its manifestation. Work hard to remember that and try not to question why certain things are happening in your life or why you are mixed up with certain people. When you do, push the stop button on your forehead and remember that the situation was set before you for a reason. Learn from it. Fall back on your moral reserves and remember that there are no mistakes. There are no coincidences. Everything happens for a reason. While you may not understand it or want to be a part of it at that moment, each and every time you will have gained something. So you see? Your mother was right. And you thought she just wanted to give you a hard time.

Chapter 5:

Support.

"Most of us, swimming against the tides of trouble the world knows nothing about, need only a bit of praise or encouragement - and we will make the goal." – Jerome Fleishman

Support in change can be one of the most difficult things to come by. When you can't find it with friends or family you have absolute permission to look outside the ordinary realm of people you know in order to find it. And yes, I know that sounds a bit frightening, but only for a moment.

The first time I told my father I wanted to leave my job as a web developer to go into news, he shook his head. (This was in 2001.) His reaction was the same when I told him I was leaving news altogether in 2010.

"You're making a mistake," he said.

Yes, he paid for part of my education, and yes he knew I had a degree in Radio and Television Production. That wasn't what he had a problem with. It was the fact that I was leaving my $30 thousand dollar a year job (which was a decent salary for a young, single girl at that time) for an $18 thousand dollar a year job as a television reporter in Watertown, New York.

"Sometimes, Jo, you gotta do what you don't want to. It's not about what you like. It's about the money. You have a decent job that pays you well and will continue to pay you the longer you stay on. Don't be stupid."

There was someone else in my life that also tried to dissuade me. The day I went in for my interview and to "read" for the news director, that someone else said, "Don't get your hopes up. You're going to a shit news station about the size of a postage stamp. You won't get anywhere starting there. You're just wasting your time."

But I didn't listen. Because I didn't want to. I knew what I wanted to do. And so I walked into that tiny news station with all of the huff and glory that I had. I sat down confidently at the anchor desk and reached for the floor pedal that would roll the words on the teleprompter in front of me. I read *every single word* out loud that was written on the screen – including the director's prompts. My cold read went a little something like this:

Me: "Watertown residents are concerned about their electricity bills. It seems a recent hike in gas prices has folks turning down their heat turn to camera 2."

News director: "You can just skip the director's prompts. Just read the news."

Me: "Okay." (back to teleprompter.) "Mark Black, a resident of one Watertown neighborhood, intends to do something about it roll VO."

News director: "Again, skip the director's prompts."

Me: "The stuff in parenthesis?"

News Director: "Yes. Like roll VO. That stands for voice over. You don't need to read that. The director needs to see that so he knows when to roll the video over your voice."

It's amazing the man hired me. These were things I should have known. But it had been at least seven years since I graduated with my degree in radio and television production. Because I never sought an internship while in college, there were many things I simply didn't retain. The news director let that fact fall by the wayside.

"You're a natural," he told me that day. "Not too bad for a girl that's never done this before."

Less than a week later he called me and asked if I was interested in a part-time weekend reporter position. As you already know from the first chapter, I took it. For the first year, I worked both jobs. I spent Monday through Friday as a desktop-publisher-slash-web-developer and Saturdays and Sundays as a reporter. And when the offer for a contract came (a glorious $18 thousand *plus* $250 for hair and make-up), I took it. I gave my full-time employer two-weeks notice and left my desk job to become the North Country's newest version of Brenda Starr. There was no doubt I was making the right choice. And at the time, it was *exactly* what I needed to do. There were certainly people close to me that criticized my choice. But I didn't let that shake me. Perhaps those individuals didn't support my decision to roam the streets of Watertown with a microphone in my hand, but there were some people out there who did.

Every Wednesday night I played softball with two high school friends, Stacey and Shelley Kritzer. They're twins. That has nothing to do with my story, but I think it adds color, so there you go.

Anyway, I played softball with the duo. And one fine day as I sat on the bench waiting for my turn, I confessed that I was unhappy with my job and wanted to go into local news.

"Don's a reporter in Watertown," Stacey said.

"Don? Who the hell is Don?" I asked.

"He's our cousin. The guy up to bat right now who is about to hit a home run," she said.

I looked closely at the tall, dark haired man at home plate waiting for the perfect pitch. I had played an entire season of softball with the guy and never knew he was the twins' cousin. Today (at least as I write this) he is a successful reporter at WTOC, a CBS affiliate in Savannah, Georgia.

"He's a reporter?" I asked, surprised.

"Yeah," Shelley said. "You should talk to him."

And so after the game that's just what I did.

"What kind of experience do you have?" he asked me.

"None. I never did an internship. And I think I worked one day at the radio station at the college."

"So that's your experience? That's it?"

"That's it."

He looked at me for a moment and then said, "Put a resume together for me. Jazz it up a little bit. I'll pass it along to the news director at the station."

I did just what he told me to do. I'll be honest, I didn't expect him to really help me. I didn't even really know the guy. But he stayed true to his word. Despite the fact I had no formal training in television, he passed my resume along all the same, touting my talents to the news director. It was because of Don that I got that interview where I rolled through the teleprompter reading the director's prompts aloud. Thanks to his support and a heck of a lot of confidence on my part, I got the job. And when I was offered a full-time position a year later, it was the very same people on the very same softball field who supported my decision to leave my desk job to become a reporter in the first place. It was just what I needed; hearing someone else (or two someone else's that look exactly the same) tell me it was okay to jump into the unknown. Despite the resistance I met from others my gut told me everything was going to be okay. And so did my friends.

Now I know what some of you may be thinking: That's a very nice story, Joleene. Good for you. But what about those of us who have *no* support? What do you propose we do?

Well, quite simply, you go out and you get it. It may be a complete stranger who ends up helping you. But you won't know who is willing to help if you don't take a few risks. Here's what I mean:

When I decided I wanted to speak for a living I had no idea where to start. There was no school or curriculum that specialized in inspirational speaking in my neighborhood and I had never heard of Toastmasters at the time. (Toastmasters are a non-profit organization aimed at helping people develop public speaking and leadership skills.) I wasn't ready to tell my father I planned to make another career change and quite frankly, I didn't know how to put it to other people who were asking me.

"So you're leaving news," they'd say. "Where are you going?"

"Oh, well, I intend to become an inspirational speaker. I want to change peoples lives by encouraging them to follow their dreams, goals and passions."

I could just imagine the blank stares I would get. My cousin Anne DesRosiers Killen said recently, "Learning how other people truly perceive you is uncomfortable. But what you do with that knowledge is a true test of your character."

She ain't kiddin'.

Regardless of the reaction from others, how I handled it would define me and what I was capable of. If people reacted negatively and I let them get to me, then I was really showing a lack of faith in myself. During my transition from reporter to speaker I was very afraid. I was ready and willing to make changes, but I don't deny on any level that I was scared to death of an unfavorable outcome. I needed someone that would not only support my decision, but could understand my passion for wanting *so badly* to inspire and lift people up to a whole new realm of possibility for themselves. Thanks to the constant flow of energy throughout the universe, I found her.

I was sitting at my desk in the newsroom one day envisioning myself on a stage with hundreds of people in front of me listening to my all-encompassing, powerful message, when I suddenly remembered an interview I had done with a motivational speaker at a teacher's conference in Syracuse. I searched the news station's website for the story and found it. It had been about a year since the story had aired but there it was, in all its glory. I played the video version and watched until the woman's name came up on the screen: *Anne Holiday.* As I continued to watch the story, I remembered I had intentionally asked her questions about her work outside the scope of my story in an effort to gain insight for myself. Those questions didn't make it into the final story and I didn't intend for them to; I just wanted to know more about who she was and how she got started. After the interview I had asked for her card. Now I found myself pawing through my makeshift Rolodex (a small, narrow box with a mish-mash of business cards crammed inside in no particular order). When I found it, I typed in her web address and looked over every page, hoping to find a bio and learn how she got started. Instead, I found a page where she sold her books. There, at the top of the page was her latest book with a description that read: *Want to be a motivational speaker and author? Now you can! Find the tools you need to build a career that will change your life and the lives of others. Learn how to author your own book, too!*

I couldn't believe it. Are you kidding me? This woman wrote a book on the two very things I wanted to conquer? And the answers to my questions were right in the book under my nose? I already had a very good handle on how to write and publish a book, thanks to three fiction attempts, several submissions of two children's books, years of reading *Writers Digest* and my own freelance work. I was a communications major in college and took public speaking classes, so I had a handle on a lot of what I was getting in to. But as far as how to bring it all full circle? *ZILCH.*

So I bought the book.

Less than a week later it arrived, greeting me at my desk when I walked into work that morning. I couldn't wait to get home to start reading it. I ripped open the packaging, eager to peek at the book. It had been shipped locally. The address on the business card stuffed inside was also local. When I met her the year before, I figured she had been flown in from the West Coast. I mean, isn't that where all motivational speakers and authors live? On the West Coast? The fact she was from Central New York thrilled me even more. That made me realize that I could achieve greatness anywhere, at anytime.

I dove into that book as soon as I got home, reading every page as to not miss a beat. Then I got to a section of suggested steps offered by Holiday that could bring me closer to my goal. Many were steps I had already taken on my own. But the last suggestion really got the wheels turning: *Write a letter to an organization or individual and ask for help.*

I stopped reading and pondered this. Ask for help? Ask who for help? Anyone? Anne Holiday herself, perhaps? I laughed at the very thought. But then I sat back in my chair, holding my chin, thinking, *why not?* The worst thing she could do is say no. She doesn't know me and I don't know her, right? So why not?

I proceeded to write an email to Mrs. Anne Holiday, motivational speaker, author and Central New York resident. I told her I had reached the point in her book where she recommended we do different things to get us closer to our goal, one of which was writing a letter asking for help.

"And so I'm asking you for yours, Mrs. Holiday," I wrote. "All I want is one hour of your time, nothing more, nothing less, just one hour to talk to me about how you got started. I would love to hear your story."

Three days later she emailed me back. Yes, she would meet with me. I was *so* excited! This was *GREAT!* I had pushed enough to get myself in front of someone who has been writing and speaking for years. We met at a coffee shop near her home. Anne and I hit it off immediately. We talked about laughter and love and the local media. I bought her lunch and we talked even longer than the promised hour. Before I left, she asked me a question that still blows my mind when I think about it today.

"Would you be interested in speaking in front of hundreds of women at a conference with me next year?"

My jaw dropped.

This woman had never heard me speak. Other than high school classrooms on Career Day and in my living room with Sydney-dog, my words and inspirational fire had never been felt or heard by anybody. Why was she asking me this? Is she insane?

"Why are you asking me to speak? You've never even heard me do it. How do you know I can?"

"I have a feeling you'd be just fine," she said. "It will give you the practice you need and give me a speaker who some people out there just might be familiar with."

Anne admitted she had never actually seen me on the news, but that didn't mean anything. She was smart enough to realize I could be recognizable to many Central New Yorkers - and I was smart enough to bite.

And so I agreed. Putting together and being a part of a conference for Christian women was one of the most amazing journeys I have ever been a part of. Not only did I speak before 422 women of faith, I also acted as conference director, which allowed me to play a huge role in putting it all together. I still shake my head at the thought of this. If I hadn't sent Anne that email, I never would have experienced what I did. I'm quite certain I would have found my way as a speaker in time, but I believe everything happens for a reason and my encounter with Anne was *supposed* to happen. I gained tremendous insight as a program director. I wrote my first real presentation for that day, too, practicing it in front of Anne well in advance so she could give me pointers. I also gained a friend. Anne and I became pretty tight in the months leading up to the conference. The conference is now an annual event for Christian women looking to connect or reconnect with their faith. And while I'm not Christian myself, spending time with the volunteers and Anne during the planning stage taught me plenty. I read most of the Bible (the Old Testament and the New Testament) and asked plenty of questions. I also experienced six different women laying their hands on me, praying that I didn't pass a kidney stone the day of the conference. (I had been to the emergency room twice in the days leading up to the event.) I had experienced opportunity that I never would have imagined or anticipated, all because I approached a complete stranger that was willing to give her time to me. I will always be grateful to Anne for believing in me and opening her heart to me.

Cheryl Richardson, an author, coach and speaker featured in the movie, *You Can Heal Your Life* said, "Don't go to the hardware store for milk. Turn to people for support that are really going to support you."

I'm sure many of us have faced challenges and tackled them head on flying solo. But if you think about it, there was some kind of support *somewhere* during that journey. Even if it was someone saying the right thing at the right time, it was there. Words of encouragement feed you. And when someone lets you know they are *really* there, it can make all the difference in the world.

No one else knows what you were put on this earth to accomplish except for *you*. Having said that, keep one thing in mind and shove it to the forefront every time you meet resistance: regardless of the change you want to make, how you want to make it and why, you will almost always, unequivocally, meet the disapproval of others. Somebody, somewhere, will give you reasons why you shouldn't leave your current job or end a tumultuous relationship. They will tell you that spending your inheritance to write a novel or take a summer off to live in England is insane. They will assure you that running for office is a waste of time and energy, and how selfish can you be, anyway? They will foo-foo your idea to adopt a child from a third world country while making it very clear they disagree with your decision to give away half your furniture to the family that recently lost their house in a fire. They will tell you that you can't. Interestingly enough, in the words of Wayne Dyer, the fact that they tell you that you can't is *their* limitation. Not yours. So go for it. That's what I say.

Chapter 6:

Follow the signs.

"Your mind knows only some things. Your inner voice, your instinct, knows everything. If you listen to what you know instinctively, it will always lead you down the right path." – Henry Winkler

When I was very young, probably eight or nine years old, I made a tiny little magazine out of lined paper I found stuffed in a drawer of my mother's desk. I carefully cut the paper into small squares and stapled it together along the left side. Then I decorated each page with eye-catching phrases and pictures. I drew some of them, but mostly I cut them out of magazines to glue inside. Then I walked boldly into my big brothers room and announced, "I'm going to be publishing this magazine once a month. You can buy a copy every month for ten cents."

"I don't want that stupid thing," he scoffed. He aimed his Star Wars Boba Fett action figure at the magazine and made shooting sounds with his mouth.

"But it took me a long time to make it!"

He grabbed the magazine out of my hands and thumbed sloppily through the pages. "This is stupid."

"You're buying it," I said.

"No, I'm not!" He shoved the tiny magazine back at me.

"Oh yes you are!"

"You can't make me!" he shouted.

"If you don't buy this magazine from me every month for at a dime, I'm telling Mom about the Sears models you cut out of her catalog and glue onto paper so you can look at it at night."

He immediately produced a dime.

I didn't realize it at the time, but this scenario was one of many signs I would experience (yet not immediately understand the significance of) throughout my life that would point me in the direction of what I was meant to do. And there was *lots* I wanted to do. I wanted to be a singer and an actress and a writer. I wanted to make movies and star in movies and make and edit the previews for my movies. I wanted to be a novelist and a screenwriter and Neil Simon's protégé. I wanted to be famous and have everyone know who I was. There was *so much* I wanted, as a matter of fact, that when I was a young adult I became completely stressed out about it because I didn't know which path to follow. So I tried a little bit of everything. I went to Onondaga Community College for Radio and Television Production and then moved on to Niagara University where I studied Theatre. After graduating from Niagara in 1996, I toured the east coast with a theatre company out of Philadelphia for a season and then came home to contemplate life. I loved being on stage, that was for sure. So I auditioned for a local production of *Chess*, only to be severely disappointed to learn the production was cancelled due to budget concerns. But I forged on. Every week I would scour the *Syracuse New Times* looking for audition opportunities. I even perused the section where band members were looking for other band members. It was there I found an ad from a band looking for a new female vocalist. I knew in my gut that I could easily front a band. And so I called for an audition.

Over the next four years, I sang as the front man for three different bands in and around the Syracuse area. (These were the years that I spent as a desktop-publisher-slash-web-developer.) I was young, single and full of fire. By day I did the layout for a musical instrument and accessories catalog, and by night I was belting out tunes at various bars or weddings, daydreaming of becoming the next Sheryl Crow. I was following my heart. My gut. My instincts. My passions. And while I couldn't narrow them down to just one, I kept doing whatever my little mind told me to do. I didn't realize it at the time, but every step I took was leading me directly to where I am now. Every song, every state I traveled through with the theatre company, every page I laid out in the magazine and every page I updated on the web; every live shot I did and every story I wrote in the news business and every – single - *damn* heartbreak I dealt with prepared me for *now*. Even in that swirl of uncertainty that seemed to last for years, I continued to forge ahead do what my heart told me to do. When I look back on this process, I'm amazed at how far I've really come. There were days I stumbled through, sometimes intoxicated, other times hungry as hell. There were nights I cried relentlessly at the demons that gripped me and early mornings where I would just lay awake and wonder what was next. But somehow, no matter if it was light or dark, I kept moving forward, even if it was a little bit. I spent at least five years (from 2005 – 2009) frozen with fear and still managed to move a tiny bit forward each day. Something tells me if you were to inventory your life in the same way, you would discover the same thing about yourself. Even during the most tumultuous time in your life, you were somehow moving forward.

Moving forward doesn't mean it is only affective if it's happening at lightning speed. You can move as slow as a tortoise and still make progress. There are days when you can only do so much, too. When those days come along, remind yourself you did the best you could for that day. Because you really did. That's my husbands philosophy, anyway. And I dig it.

Now lets fast-forward to 2010, the end of my ten-year reign as a reporter. Yes, I busted my butt the entire time I worked as a reporter, but after ten years the need for growth and change was stronger than I had ever remembered. It pulled at me and yanked at me and nagged at me regularly. I knew that if I didn't listen to my gut, my inner voice, I knew if I didn't make change and follow my heart, that I would live in a world where I was unhappy all the time. It would be the same world that so many of us live in now; a world where work is a ball and chain and Monday is the most dreaded day across the land; a place where there are bright spots, but no bright days. It's the light of the Universe that gives us those bright days. And I could no longer deny myself that light. I thought the regret of not following through with my passions would be more painful and frightening than staying "stuck" in my job.

The idea of making change kept me up at night and made me cry more than I thought any one human being could do. I was frazzled and frustrated. But when I stopped and thought about everything I had ever done there was one underlying theme that played a part in all of it: Writing.

I wrote songs and plays and short stories. I had novel ideas that I began, but never finished. I wrote news stories and investigative series pieces. I even wrote a pilot for a sitcom about my gay college roommate and me. He was gay and happy; I was straight and miserable. I actually wrote three episodes of this seemingly witty comedy but never did anything with it, mostly because I didn't know how. About two years after I set the scripts aside, a smash-hit comedy called *Will and Grace* hit the airwaves. I always wondered if I had more gumption, knowledge and drive, would I have tackled the first gay-guy-living-with-a-straight-girl sitcom? Don't get me wrong here, *Will and Grace* was spectacular and had amazing writers. I was just a girl writing in my bedroom at night. The point is that I had something halfway decent and didn't do anything with it. There was even the time I wrote a story for *Cosmopolitan* magazine. I was seventeen years old. I remember asking my mother to copy-edit it for me (yet I'm sure I didn't use that terminology because I certainly didn't know what the hell it meant at the time) before I sent it in. She checked it for grammatical errors and gave it back to me. I re-wrote the entire story again, longhand, and sent it to the editor. I'm pretty sure the staff at *Cosmopolitan* had a good laugh when they saw my hand-written story upon opening the envelope. And if they *did* take the time to read it and the title *Michael's Nightmare* didn't kill them, I imagine my feeble attempt at writing a steamy love story certainly did.

Let me go on about my love of writing. Part of it has to do with a strange attraction to blank journals. I can remember as far back as twenty years now, going directly to the wall in any given bookstore to look over the selection. I loved to look at how they were put together. I would touch them first to feel what kind of material they were made of. Some were leather; others were bound in colorful materials. The pages inside the journals varied. Some had lines to guide the writer, others did not. No matter how they were constructed, I loved thumbing through the crispness of the paper, smelling the pages as they buzzed across my nose. To this day, the blank journal wall is still my first stop in a bookstore. And I own plenty of those little books, too. I use some as personal journals while others are strictly for notes when I read or write. I buy handmade one-of-a-kind journals to keep for my daughter. I imagine someday she'll pull out these special books to read how our lives unfolded together.

Without ever realizing it, all of these scenarios throughout the years were signs for me. For the most part, I unintentionally ignored them. But not entirely, and not on purpose. Sometimes you've got to get hit in the head with a brick before you recognize what life has put before you. My brick hit me in the face the day I was reading Dan Millman's book, *The Life you were Born to Live*. Remember the pain-filled joy I talked about in the introduction? That's what I felt when it became clear that what I wanted to do with my life was actually part of my DNA. It finally hit me. That's what you'll experience when you become "clear" on what you want to do with your life. So how do you make that happen? I'm convinced that it's different for everybody and that it will hit you when least expect it. You'll be doing something or looking at something or reading something and it will just *hit* you. In the meantime, you can forge a path for your brain to follow. The trick is to consider the signs. If you were to take inventory of all the things you enjoy or are attracted to, you would see a pattern emerge. From that pattern, different ideas will follow. That's when it starts to become clear. Pause for a moment and consider this. What *are* you attracted to? Find a piece of paper and write it down. All of it. Think about the things that you enjoy doing. If you don't think it's necessary to write it all down, think again. Sometimes seeing your interests on paper can help you recognize what actually exists *within* you. Do you like music? Are you attracted to different kinds of music? To music stores? To pianos or guitars? Do you like to listen to live music? Write it down. Or maybe you enjoy helping others. Do you find yourself always looking out for those around you? Do you help the older folks in the store? Are you patient with them? Do you volunteer a lot? Where do you volunteer? Write it down. Do you watch any TV? What do you watch on TV? What kinds of shows are you eager to see? Crime shows? Cooking shows? Car shows? Fashion or style shows? What about the reality shows that have collectors scouring the country for antiques? Anything like that? Even if your thoughts and interests are not related to one another, write them down anyway. Maybe you like to tinker with cars or build things. Maybe you like to bake and own more cookbooks than you know what do to with. Write it down. Do you like to play poker? Write it down. Do you like to run? Write it down. Do you like to draw or do pottery or turn old, junky treasures into shiny, new ones? Write it down. Give yourself several days to collect these thoughts, too. They won't all come at once. But, they will come.

I like to tell a story now and again about a woman named Gloria. Gloria worked at a local bank as a teller. She was seemingly happy, or so she thought, but when the economy tanked she lost her job. Gloria wasn't married at the time and never had children. She only had to worry about fending for herself. When she became unemployed she kept busy in two ways: actively seeking work in the newspapers and mulling around yard sales and flea markets. Gloria would pick up random items like porcelain dolls or small bits of furniture and fix them up like new. Then she would turn around and sell them on eBay or craigslist. She really enjoyed it too. It kept her busy and got her creative juices flowing. And so she kept on doing it. Slowly but surely, she began making money. Her days were soon filled with creativity and hard work, although she didn't feel burdened by it. She would bargain hunt in the early morning hours and paint and hammer and stain and finish in the afternoons. When her older brother saw the potential she had, he suggested she push it full boar and go into business for herself. It was an idea that never crossed her mind. But when her brother offered to help her with a website and start-up costs, she became electrified with the very thought. She *loved* what she was doing. Her days were filled with creativity and passion. She agreed to jump into the unknown and follow through. She would call her business *Glorified Treasures*.

A few short weeks after she made this very courageous decision, Gloria ran into an old friend. When that old friend asked her how things were, Gloria was thrilled to answer.

"I'm gong to start my own business selling refurnished items," she explained to her friend. "After I got laid off, I started wandering around flea markets. I would buy stuff real cheap and take it home to fix up. Then I would turn around and sell it online for a profit. My brother is helping me get started. I'm so excited about this!"

Her friend was less than thrilled.

"You can't do that," she told Gloria. "That's not the way it works. You have to work a real job just like everybody else, whether you like it or not. Why should you get to play with arts and crafts whenever you feel like it and not work like everybody else? You need to get a real job and quit messing around."

Because she was teetering on the cusp of something exciting but still frightening, Gloria fell back into the realm of fear and took her friends words as gospel. She dropped the idea of starting her business refinishing furniture and other treasures and eventually took a job as a mortgage lender.

Now this is the part of the story that I love: about three weeks into her new job, Gloria said she literally stood up from her desk and looked around her little office. Nothing in it made her happy, not the pictures on the wall or the plants in the corner. Not the friendly woman in the office across from her who always had a dish full of chocolates or the extremely accommodating man who hired her. *Nothing.* She wanted to do what she loved: tear things apart and build them up to be bigger and better and prettier. And so she walked into her bosses office and politely told him she wasn't happy. Amazingly, he understood and let her go without a grudge. He even guided her to a non-profit organization in the county that could help her put a business plan together at no cost. Within three months, Gloria was doing business as *Glorified Treasures* and still is today.

After Gloria told me this story I asked her if she had always been sort of crafty. She said she had been, all her life, but never really pushed it or pondered it. She enjoyed moments where she was involved in such projects, but didn't think she could support herself with her talents. Once she became clear and followed her heart, things began to change. And when she became clear about what she wanted, doors opened for her that she never even knew existed.

You can have, do or be *anything* you want. The first time I heard that phrase it came out of the mouth of Jack Canfield, author of *Chicken Soup for the Soul.* Actually, I've heard lots of authors say that. In writing this book, I wanted to learn who the original author of that statement was, not only to give them credit, but because it's so very true and so very powerful. After doing some research, I thought that Abraham Lincoln came the closest to owning the affirmation:

"You can have anything you want - if you want it badly enough. You can be anything you want to be, do anything you set out to accomplish if you hold to that desire with singleness of purpose."

If you know anything about the life and times of our 16th president, you know he failed in business early in his adult life. In 1832 he ran for the Illinois legislature but was defeated. That same year he lost his job and couldn't go to law school. He declared bankruptcy shortly thereafter, spending the next two decades of his life paying off the debt. None of this stopped him from doing what he wanted. In 1835 his fiancé died. He suffered a nervous breakdown and it's said he spent nearly six months in bed. But you know what? He eventually got up. He got up and walked out the door and ran for congress. Did he win? Nope. He was defeated. Three years later he ran again. Did he prevail then? Nope. He was again defeated. Two years after that, he ran *again* – and *again,* he was defeated. In 1854 he decided to take another shot at politics. He won a slot into the Illinois legislature, but declined the seat, hoping instead to become a U.S. Senator.

After so many losses, most people would have given up. They would have taken their ball and bat and just gone home. But not Abe. He ran for President in 1856 and once again, he was defeated. He tried another run for senate a few years later and guess what? He *lost.*

In 1860, everything changed. After several shots at different political offices, Lincoln won on the big ticket and became the 16th president of these United States. I neglected to mention he lost his mother and his sister before he even began his venture as a politician. Despite all of his losses, both personal and political, the man did not lie down and die. He may have paused for a while, but he never threw in his tall trademark hat. Not only should his story impress you, it should inspire you and remind you that you have the power to have, do and be anything you want. *ANYTHING*. We all do. Every single one of us.

Don't be fooled by a string of stories like mine that may give you the illusion that all I have experienced is sunshine and glory. While I choose to bask in the positive outcomes as much as possible, there were and still are days that roll on without a sign from God or the Universe that everything will be okay. But the energy is still working, still moving in and around me, just like it moves in and around you. Just because what you're waiting for doesn't appear before you at the very moment *you* think it should, doesn't mean it isn't going to arrive. Remember – there is no such thing as instant gratification. The Universal Spirit hears you and will bring it to you. You'll know when it's arrived because your gut will tell you it has arrived. Then you must act. Without action, you're only waiting for a rainbow that will never appear. So listen. And trust what you're hearing. Yes, finding that trust will take time. But, when the day comes that everything you asked for and worked for comes to fruition, you will smile uncontrollably and thank God for being so patient and giving. You will see the result of your faith and your passions come alive before you. Hang onto that undeniable feeling of bliss for as long as you can. Because *that's* the feeling you are working to attain and bring into your life every – single – day.

Chapter 7:

Letting Go.

"There's no need to miss someone from your past. There's a reason they didn't make it to your future." – Unknown

I have a tumultuous relationship with a certain family member. It's grown especially harsh the past few years. I believe it has to do with a rage he has allowed to build up inside of him for years and years. I'm quite certain he would tell you different. Despite his thoughts or my thoughts, one thing is certain; I have a healthier life without him.

Like me, he suffers from addiction. Alcohol is his primary poison. I want desperately to break through to him, but he won't let me in. I've tried. Believe me. But this isn't about who did what and why – this is about letting go of what you can't change so that you can focus on changing the things you can.

When my mother told me years ago there would be things in my life that would cause me pain in ways I couldn't imagine, I didn't know what she was talking about. I was a teenager, and the only pain I suffered was the occasional break-up with a boyfriend or getting slapped across the face by her if I was mouthy. I didn't know I would feel the pain of having a poor relationship with someone so close to me. When he looks at me with hatred I can feel my heart tighten as it falls into my stomach. I want to kick and scream and yell. And then I do what I do best in these kinds of situations: I cry. I cry for all that has happened and all that I can't change. I cry for my daughter because she is also affected. She can't have a relationship with him because I don't think it's healthy. Because I keep her at bay, it makes him that much more angry. There's lots of anger. There is *so much* anger in this area of my life that it often stops me dead in my tracks. Within seconds, I can go from lucrative and happy to somber and still. All of this, of course, affects me tremendously. And the more I let it affect me, the more I pull backward. It took me a very long time before I discovered there was only so much I could do. Once I did all of that, I had to give it up to the skies above.

There was a point in my life where every single day was dark and hope was only a four-letter word. During that time I worked as a mortgage lender and I met someone then that told me something I would hang onto and use much later in my life. That someone is a wonderful man named John Birkmier. John trained me during my time as a loan officer. He is a man of God and believe me when I tell you, if he's got it, he'll give it to you. One day as I sat in his office crying the blues about the struggles I was going through he said, "You gotta give it up to God. Just hand it over to him."

I looked at him surprised. "I don't know how to do that," I mumbled through my tears. "How do I do that?"

"Realize there is nothing more you can do about the situation. You've done all you can. Now let it go. Let God drive for a while."

I raised my eyebrows at the very thought. How could I let something just – go? I was so used to internalizing everything that the very idea of giving it to the Cosmos seemed unreal. I left his office with a polite "Thank You" and went back to my own. I have to admit that I sat there for a very long time wondering how I was supposed to give my problems over to God. I visualized them leaving my head in a white cloud of smoke and heading upward. But I still felt the same. Try as I might, I could not release what I was struggling with. It wasn't until years later that his advice made sense to me.

I was in zumba class one night when it happened, dancing happily away, thrilled with how I was nailing every step of every dance. The music was loud and fun and had all of us on fire. I was smiling out loud, living in the moment when the words, *There's nothing more you can say or do. Let it go,* ran through my head. Still not missing a beat, I smiled differently now. Tears came to my eyes. At that very moment, I gave up my struggle with my family member. I don't know why it happened in the middle of a zumba class or what triggered it; all I know is that there were tears of relief as I danced. The conversation between John Birkmier and myself ran through my mind.

"So *this* is what he was talking about. *This* is what he meant," I thought.

At a most unusual moment, I was able to let it go. The Divine Force above me was ready and willing to take it. I realized as I step-ball-changed my way through the evening, that I had done everything I believed I could to mend fences with my relative. The burden was no longer mine to carry. I felt lighter and happier and so I danced even harder.

I've thought about that night at least a hundred times since it's happened. It's clear that the energy force at work aligned with me at the very moment it believed I was ready, removing layers of pain and frustration that I couldn't conquer. The trick, I realized, was making that happen with other issues I internalized. I had to be ready to let go. I had to be ready to realize that there was nothing more I could do about the situation and close the door on it. There are times I know this but I still cling to things that have happened and make them all my own. Why, I don't know. Why do any of us make situations outside of our control *our* problem? Insecurity plays a huge part, which is why learning to love ourselves can be difficult. But it is so crucial. It is, without a doubt, the single most important thing you can do for yourself. It's something you can teach your children right now. I'm no parenting expert, but there's one thing I do know: teaching youngsters in our lives that we are *all the same* and should be accepted *without judgment* can lay the foundation for a more stable child; one that will grow to love and accept themselves and others just the way they are. Because of the world we live in today, there is no doubt this isn't easy. Again, we are surrounded by ideas of perfection all the time. But remember: change is progressive and nothing happens overnight.

I was recently hired to write an article for a business owner not far from my home. Summer vacation had just begun so Madison was with me during the day. We drove up north, both lost comfortably in our own little worlds. I had the radio on so I could sing softly as I drove and Maddie was tucked away in the backseat with her little coat draped over her head so the sun wouldn't black out the screen of her Nintendo DS. As I approached the general area where the secretary told me the business was located, I looked at the clock. 12:56 p.m. My interview was at 1 o'clock, so I would be right on time. The intersection where I thought the business was located was right in front of me. But as I drove on through, I didn't see it. I also noticed the roads that intersected weren't the ones the secretary mentioned. Yet I was sure I was in the right location. I immediately panicked and picked up my phone to call my husband. He grew up in the area, so he would know exactly where I was supposed to be. The phone just rang and rang. Frustrated, I hung up and turned around in a parking lot. *Where did the roads she mentioned come together?* I was mad at myself because I should have known exactly where I was, too. I was a reporter in the North Country for almost four years and had been in this area dozens of times. But now I was drawing a blank. I simply couldn't find it. What I should have done was plug in my GPS and let it take me there. But I thought I was so close, I would just stumble upon it. I looked at the clock. 1:10 p.m. Not good. I dialed the number to the business. The secretary that answered was less than thrilled.

"This is Joleene Moody. I have an appointment with Mr. and Mrs. Businessowners for 1 o'clock. But I'm lost."

"Your *lost*," she said in disbelief. I thought her tone was edgy and rude and it upset me even more.

"Yes. I'm lost," I said. "I was supposed to be there ten minutes ago -"

"We know. One o'clock."

"Yes. And it's 1:10. I know. And I apologize. But I'm having trouble locating you."

"Where are you?" she asked me dryly.

I looked around me.

"I'm at the intersection of Routes 1 and 2. I passed Route 3 but I don't see where 1 and 3 actually intersect."

Clearly making it obvious that I was an idiot, she again explained where the business was.

"Thank you," I said as politely as possible. "I'll be there in a few minutes. I'm literally two minutes away. I'm so sorry."

She hung up without saying anything. Her actions frustrated me even more, setting the tone for the rest of my lost drive. Madison sat quietly in the back seat, still huddled under her little coat playing her DS.

"Mom's frustrated, Maddie. But not with you, okay?"

"Okay," she said.

"I may swear. A lot."

"Yes, Mom." She was preoccupied with her game.

And so I headed in the direction the secretary told me. I found nothing. I stopped at a hotel and went inside to ask for directions. The kindly woman behind the counter told me where I needed to go. As I headed in the direction she suggested, I still didn't see the business. I was on the verge of going over the edge when my phone rang. It was Mark.

"I can't find this damn place," I said near tears. It was 1:30 now. I was officially a half an hour late. He tried to calm me, but to no avail. I hung up with him and called the office again, only to be greeted by an answering machine. I was mad at my foolishness for not knowing where I was and certain that if and when I *did* find the building, I would come face to face with some very angry people. In all of my years as a journalist, I was rarely late. There were some instances, yes, but I never remember being this tardy. Nor did I ever suffer an attitude like that of the woman I had just hung up with. She appeared very unforgiving at the 10-minute mark. I could only imagine what she would be like at the 30-minute mark.

Just then, the building appeared before me on my left. And it was nowhere near the intersection she told me. (Seriously.) I yanked my car into the driveway just as another car pulled out. I had a sinking feeling that Mr. and Mrs. Businessowner were behind the wheel of that car. I pulled up in front of an open door where a very angry looking woman sat at a desk glaring at me from inside.

"Stay here, Maddie," I said.

"Yes, Mom," she answered. She knew I was on the edge.

"Hi there," I said as I walked into the tiny office where the woman sat smugly. "I'm Joleene Moody. And I'm so sorry I'm late. I just couldn't find the place."

She didn't care. She hated me. She was stabbing my heart with invisible daggers and dragging my body through endless acres of mud.

"They're not here anymore," she said with a cool grin. "They got tired of waiting and they left."

"I'm so sorry. I don't know what to say. I called again, but no one answered the phone. I just – I was lost."

"You called a second time?" She looked around her desk for the phone as if it had moved. "I've been sitting here. I get a hundred calls or more a day. Do you have any idea how busy I am? I am busier that you have ever been at the busiest time in your life. And Mr. and Mrs. Businessowners are busy, too. And why wouldn't they be? They own four businesses. Do you have any idea what I had to go through to get them here today? In the same place? It was no easy task."

"I imagine," I said, biting my tongue. I didn't want confrontation. I wanted peace. I wanted her to see that I truly didn't mean to be late. But she wasn't interested.

"Oh, you have no idea," she retorted.

"Again, I apologize. It wasn't intentional. I got lost. I didn't mean to, but I did. I realize I'm a half hour late and they've left. Perhaps we can talk about rescheduling? Again, it was an honest mistake."

"They sat here the entire time asking me where you were," she continued. "They were very angry at me because it takes quite a bit to get them both here at the same time. They run four businesses, you know. And I'm very busy myself - always busy. They also had a meeting at 1:30 and now they're late for that meeting because you're late."

It was obvious that this woman didn't want to hear my apology. I also believed she was embellishing a bit to make me feel even worse. I had originally asked her the day before to block out a half-hour for the interview. That would mean giving me 1-1:30. If the couple *really* had a second meeting and they were seasoned business owners, wouldn't they have scheduled it *after* 1:30 and not *at* 1:30 - to allow for drive time?

I was angry and only getting angrier. Not just with her, but with myself. I didn't want to feel this way. I didn't want confrontation. I just wanted her to let it go and move on. She didn't want to.

"Look," I finally said with a bit of an edge, "I'm not going to grovel anymore. I was late, I realize that, but there is nothing I can do. It is what it is. I can't go back a half-hour to change it and I can't say I'm sorry any more than I have. It was a mistake, an honest mistake. Haven't you ever made a mistake? Because that's all this was, a mistake."

"Oh, I'm sure it was. You know, I sit here all day answering phones and putting out fires and this is just one more that I have to deal with – "

I let her drone on again. I was looking right at her but not really hearing her. I peeked over my shoulder to my car where Maddie was watching me. She knew I was unhappy. I turned back to the woman who was using her hands to talk now, but I didn't hear a word she was saying. I was hearing myself say, *She wants to go on like this, Joleene. Let her. But don't allow her to get under your skin. This is who she is. Let it be and then let it go.* When I tuned back in she was saying, " - so you just tell your editor that we're not interested."

"I'll do that. Thank you," I said curtly and I walked out the door. I had never met such unprofessionalism in all my life. I was dumbfounded. I tried desperately to hold my anger so my daughter wouldn't see it. But that little kid is brilliant. She knows me.

"Maddie," I said as I got back in the car.

"Yes, Mom?"

"Don't ever let anyone treat you poorly."

"Yes, Mom."

Even in my frustration, I realize I shouldn't have said that to Maddie. I guess I wanted her to know my anger wasn't directed toward her. More than that, I really wanted her to be respected all the days of her life. I never want anyone to speak to her negatively. I might as well put her in a plastic bubble.

Evolution of one's self is a practice. It takes time. It takes instances just like the one I told you about to hone the skills of acceptance and non-judgment. I clearly failed that day because I judged the situation and the woman sitting behind the desk. I even anticipated how I thought my editor would react when I told him he wouldn't have the story. Fortunately he didn't react the way I played it out in my mind. But all in all, I realized I had to turn things around. I couldn't let a little instance like this one get to me. I had to let it go. It didn't matter what the secretary thought of me, nor did it matter what unfolded in the moments that were now behind me. If the woman didn't want to accept my apology, that was her point of contention, not mine. I did all I could to mend the situation. Now it was time to move on. I also had to remember that I didn't know anything about this woman. For all I knew, she was suffering things in her life that caused her to be this angry, things that we can't even begin to imagine. Plato said, "Be kind, for everyone you meet is fighting a hard battle." I know what my battle is, but I have no idea what is involved with hers. Realizing this, I was able to let my anger go.

Two days later I was back on the same road, driving to the same business I couldn't find a few days prior. I was going to attempt the interview again. My editor had called the angry woman and managed to smooth things over. He told me he would assign another writer if I desired but I said no, I would keep the assignment. I needed to prove I had indeed let my anger go.

When I walked back in, the same woman was sitting in the same chair with the same angry look on her face. She just glared at me. I turned away from her and moved toward a desk where a man was sitting. I introduced myself and was brought to a table where I sat down with Mr. and Mrs. Businessowner. The interview went very well and there was no mention of what transpired a few days before. When the interview was over I walked out the door, past the glaring woman, leaving the entire incident in my past.

Too often we allow people with toxic attitudes or feelings toward us hinder our thoughts or our progression as we move forward in our lives. Even a small, negative interaction like the one with the secretary can leave a bad taste in our mouths. Often we take these interactions personally. If we dwell on the way the individual made us feel, we find ourselves questioning who we are and what we're made of. We may even go so far as to question the reality of what we're doing. The interaction with the secretary made me question my ability to delegate my own anger. That, in turn, made me wonder if I had the stuff an inspirational speaker is made of. Inspirational people are supposed to be full of love and hope and smiles at all times, right? So was I allowed to be angry at the fact this woman was angry with me? Absolutely. What I had to realize was that I had every right to experience my feelings. I just had to let them go and then let her go when I was done.

I'm on Twitter and I follow a man from Sydney, Australia named Ivan Kelly. He recently posted, "If others reject you, thank them and be grateful. You'll attract others of a more kindred spirit." I love that message. If we carefully nudge the toxic and unkind people out of our way, it leaves plenty of room for more kind and loving people to help us on our journey. That doesn't mean we turn our backs on those who don't resonate well with us, however. We are all the same. We're made of the same cosmic stuff. Therefore we need to keep these people in our hearts and minds. Someday they may do the same for you.

In a strange way that may not always make sense, everyone we meet has something to give us: a lesson to be learned or a gift to be grateful for. When they are done serving a purpose in our lives, they move on. The purpose they serve may not be readily clear. It may never be clear. The parting of ways may not always be friendly, either. But once the connection is severed we must move forward and let them move forward as well. No worries with this. It's all good. Make room for kindred spirits.

Chapter 8:

Now is a really good time.

"You are never too old to set another goal or to dream a new dream." – C.S. Lewis

There is a woman I know named Mary Randazzo. She and her husband Phil are the proprietors of Coyote Moon Vineyards in the Thousand Islands. Phil hired me in 2010 as the vineyard's very own pocket freelance writer. One of the first projects he tasked me with was to write about every person who worked at the vineyard. Once finished, the stories would be published on the Coyote Moon website and again in the local newspaper, the Thousand Islands Sun.

"Start with my wife Mary," he told me. "She's a local landmark artist. Write about her first."

And so I did. I drove through the ice and snow of the North Country a few days later and waited patiently for Mary in the back office of the vineyard. She walked in a few moments later, glowing brighter than I think I've ever seen anyone glow. She wore a white fur coat on her shoulders, furry, brown boots decked with Indian needlepoint on her feet, and remained hatless to allow her full head of flaming red hair to be seen without hindrance. At 65, Mary defies her age completely. She settled in the chair next to me, telling me immediately about a book she had just finished reading. Had I read it? No? I really should. It's fantastic. It's about a little boy who claims he met Jesus when he was sick. Did I get here okay? How was the drive? Did it take me a while? No? Well that was good. Are we ready to start the interview? Yes. Ready.

I took out my tiny tape recorder and notebook as she pulled off her white coat. I was half expecting to hear a story come out of her mouth that was rather typical: *"I've always wanted to paint, ever since I was a little girl. I used to paint on the walls and the bed and the floors and the counters..."*

But the story I got was much different.

Once upon a time Mary and Phil Randazzo lived in California. Phil owned a chain of hair salons and Mary was a hairdresser. One day as she was driving through a canyon she drove up over a hill and back down into a valley. There, in a field off to her right she saw a giant, beautiful, majestic tree.

"I decided at that moment that I wanted to paint that tree," Mary said to into my tiny recorder. "I had never picked up a brush before, but I always wanted to. So I thought that tree would be the first thing I would paint. I even had a camera in the car, sitting on the passengers seat right next to me."

But a list of errands had her focused on getting into town and taking care of them. So she drove past the field with the giant tree and onward toward her destination. She made a few extra stops and even visited a friend. When her errands were done Mary got back into her truck and headed home. She drove back toward the canyon, up over the other side of the hill and down into the valley. There, in the field below, she saw the tree – lying on its side now, and no longer looking very majestic. Apparently county workers had cut it down. Mary was awestruck.

"I laughed and cried at the same time," she said. "I just couldn't believe it. I laughed because isn't that just the way things go for me. I cried because once again I was a day late and a dollar short."

Mary decided at that very moment that she wasn't going to wait for anything anymore. She put her truck in drive and pulled back onto the roadway. She drove directly to an art store where she purchased paint, brushes and canvass. She also bought books that would help her learn to paint. When Mary did this she was 40-years-old. She's 65 today and she just won her first set of awards for her artwork. One of her prints hangs proudly in Larry King's office and another on the wall of the postmasters' office in Washington, D.C. I would end this paragraph with a really punchy phrase or quote, but I don't think I need to. The story speaks for itself.

New thought author Wallace Wattles said the purpose of life for man is growth; and without some kind of forward progress, life becomes unendurable. Wattles published an amazing book in 1911 called *The Science of Being Great.* He was considered one of the forefathers of self-mastery and studied the wisdom of the world's religious leaders and philosophers of his time in an effort to bring a simple and thought-provoking truth to people like you and me: people that wish to make the most of themselves by understanding that the power of the mind will get us there. Wattles writes that the power of positive thought and self-esteem are the only true measure of a person's greatness. His words are "…for the men and women, young or old, who wish to make the most of life by making the most of themselves." Even today, his words are powerful and compelling and quite frankly, in my humble opinion, will enhance your life more than any other read I can think of. When I go through periods of negativity or uncertainty I defer to the writings of this amazing author. If you've never read any of his work, I encourage you to do so. His books are quick, thought provoking reads.

Wattles says that too often we believe that lack of circumstance keeps us from doing what we really want to do. We tell ourselves a litany of things: I don't have the money. I don't have the time. I'm not in the right location. My spouse won't let me. I'm too old. All of these negative affirmations make us a slave to fear. We further this turmoil by telling ourselves what we desire is simply not attainable. Then we believe we are not worthy or good enough or even in the right place at the right time to go after it. When we fall into this thought pattern we completely lock ourselves out of what is rightfully ours. Wattles said, "Nothing is in any other man that is not in you. No man ever had more spiritual or mental power than you can attain or do greater things than you can accomplish. You can become what you want to be."

Poverty is not a bar. Heredity is not a bar. Distance or lack of money or lack of support is not a bar. If you want it, you can have it. All you have to do is change your thoughts and allow what you want to manifest in time.

As described earlier, that which we wish to have before us can be brought forth with the power of the mind. Align your thoughts with your wishes and a shift will begin to occur. I can't help but quote Wattles because he says things so simply: "The power which is in you is in the things around you. And when you move forward, things arrange themselves for your advantage. Man was formed for growth and all things external were designed for his growth."

Not long ago I was at Henninger High School in Syracuse talking to a 9th grade class about following their dreams. I made it very clear that they had the ability to do whatever they wanted in their lives and that it was theirs for the taking. When I was done talking we took poster board, scissors, glue sticks and all different kinds of magazines and made vision boards. Vision boards are used as a tool to help the creator hone in on things they would like to gain or achieve with the help of the universe. As the kids cut and pasted, the classroom teacher approached me with an article.

"Read this later," he said to me. "I shared it with the class just last week. It's about one man and how he yearned to write for years. He didn't do it until he was in his sixties. But, he eventually did it. It kind of lines up with what you talked about with the kids today."

I thanked him and tucked the article in my bag. I didn't get around to actually reading it until several weeks later. And when I did, my heart filled with joy for a man named Frank McCourt that I had never met and, unfortunately, will never have the opportunity to meet.

Frank McCourt liked pen and paper. He liked to write and would jot things down occasionally, but he never really did anything with his creations. He had big dreams to write, though. Even living in squalor as a child in Ireland, little Frankie thought he wanted to someday move to New York City and perhaps become a published author. He imagined living in the big apple with "howling traffic, elegant skyscrapers and throbbing streets". He thought he would write his way there.

"A small voice inside me told me that's what I was put on earth for and that is what I should do," McCourt wrote in a published essay. And so after he finished a stint in the Army during the Korean War, he went to New York to pursue writing.

"There I was, at last, one of millions – swimming in the dream and wondering what to do with it," he wrote. "Simple, young man. You're in America now. Ya gotta make a living, kid. Oh yes. There's garbage in America and someone has to take it out. So I slogged through dead-end jobs. I had low expectations and thought I'd be satisfied with a white-collar job and a good-humored girl I could go to the movies with and maybe marry. But that wasn't enough. So I settled for the second best choice: teaching."

McCourt taught writing for three decades in the New York City Public School system. He listened to some of his students read their work that he dubbed as genius. Sometimes McCourt would share his own writing with the class. His students would tell him he was brilliant. They would applaud him and tell him his words were magic. They would even go so far as to urge him to get published. And then:

"One day I stood before a class and found my voice weakening. I felt an epiphany coming on. I didn't want to talk anymore. I wanted to go home and make little marks on paper. I retired after thirty years of teaching and made my little marks 'til I held in my hand a book with my name on the cover. That was *Angela's Ashes*."

Frank McCourt was sixty-six years old when he wrote his first book. *Sixty-six*. The book was an instant best seller. He continued to write, "…spinning out words 'til my name was on other book covers."

Two more books followed. They were also best sellers.

I've said it twice already but I'm going to say it again: It doesn't matter who you are, how old you are, where you came from, what your income is like, whether or not you have an education, where you live, what you've done in your past, none of it matters. You can still have, do or be *anything* you want. Anything at anytime. I can't say it enough. The only limitations you face are the ones you put before you. Yes, it's frightening to make change. Yes, you will likely "stir the pot" or upset somebody in the process. Yes, you will probably make mistakes along the way. But you make mistakes anyway. So why not make them on the way to doing something really great? No doubt, someone along the way will tell you that *you can't*. And someone else may turn his or her back on you. Remember to appreciate their presence and the gift they gave you and move forward. You can move forward. You're allowed.

Making passionate, heartfelt change is indeed a journey. Like any journey, change includes the same kind of ups and downs you experience now. It's how you handle those experiences that make the difference. What was it that Lena Horne is accredited with saying? *"It's not the load the breaks you down. It's the way you carry it."*

Chapter 9:

Dealing with the fear.

"The oldest and strongest emotion of mankind is fear. And the oldest and strongest kind of fear is fear of the unknown." — H.P. Lovecraft

Moving into the unknown is scary. There is no other way to describe it. We don't like what we can't see. We like to have our cards laid out before us where we can look at all the numbers and colors. No surprises, right? But alas, that's not the way life works. It unfolds uncertain before us all the time. And when we don't want to deal with fear because we know it will bring us to our knees, we hide from it. We close the door and sit on the other side. We settle for the things we have because we can feel and touch those things and it's comfortable. There will come a point when you won't want to hide anymore. You will become curious. That's when you should work to turn fear into curiosity, as Wayne Dyer says. It's not that difficult to do, either. Not if you maybe test-drive your fear first.

Before I decided to leave my career in television, I needed to do something to prove to myself that I could leave. I needed to somehow test my own strength and see where the "fear-meter" put me. As I said before, leaving a job with all the bells and whistles to work for myself as a speaker and writer was a tough call. I felt like I needed to do something brave before I hung up my hat in TV land. So I jumped out of an airplane.

This is how it went down:

Several weeks before I actually gave my notice, I was sitting on my couch biting what was left of my nails. I was brainstorming my escape to the land of self-employment. Because I knew very little about what it was like to work for myself, I sat there frozen like a deer in headlights. I was afraid to make the first move because I didn't know what would follow. Enter my husband, his dark hair tousled and his shoes untied.

"Hey. You wanna go skydiving?" he asked me nonchalantly.

I looked up at him thinking maybe I didn't hear him right.

"What?"

"Do you want to go skydiving?" he asked again.

"Right now?"

"No, not right now," he said laughing. "In a few weeks. My Dad wants to take Charlene skydiving as a graduation gift. He wants to know if we want to go, too."

"You're shoe is untied," I said, still gnawing on my fingers.

He glanced down at his shoe and then back at me.

"If we want to go, we have to let him know so he can make reservations," he said.

Charlene is our niece on Mark's side. She is his sister Donna's oldest. Charlene usually goes by Charle (pronounced Charlie), and apparently this skydiving thing was something she really wanted to do. I, however, had no desire whatsoever to put my life in the hands of a pilot and a parachute.

"I don't think so," I said. "What if I die?"

"Your not gonna die, goof. How often do you hear about people dying because they jumped out of a plane?"

"All the time," I said.

"Really. Well, we don't have to go if you don't want to."

"Do you want to?" I asked, finally removing my fingers from my mouth.

"Yeah," he said putting his hands on his hips. "I actually do. I think it would be fun."

All of a sudden, completely out of the blue, a voice said to me, *Wait a minute. Think about this. If you can jump out of an airplane at ten thousand feet, you can do anything! You can quit your job!*

"Yeah, okay." I said. "I'll do it."

"Don't do it just because I want to do it. It's okay. We don't have to go."

"No, no. I'll go. Why not? I'm curious."

He nodded in agreement and turned on a heel to go back upstairs and call his father. (I'm happy to report he did it without tripping over his shoelaces.) I sat there wondering what the hell I just agreed to. I felt a little numb. At the time I didn't know why, but now I do. Deep in my heart I knew that I was throwing out the first pitch before really getting into the game. As crazy as it sounds, that first pitch would be the skydive. If I could jump out and make it to the ground safely, I would not only be intact to deliver my resignation, but I also would have found the courage to *actually* do it. Thereafter, I would be ready to pitch a no-hitter.

When the big day came we all piled into the car and drove two hours to a tiny airport where a very military-like pilot made it clear from the get go that he wasn't going to take any crap or snide remarks from any of us. So I was forced to keep my mouth shut. We spent about an hour sitting outside in the sun waiting for our prep class and another hour sitting inside a hot room waiting for the class to actually begin. When the pilot finally arrived, we watched as he explained where we would sit in the plane, how we would have to wiggle backward to be strapped to our instructor and how we would cross ourselves before we jumped.

"Like this?" I asked doing the sign of the cross on my forehead and chest.

"No, young lady," he responded, and not the least bit amused, "like this." He crisscrossed his arms on his chest so that his hands were on his shoulders and glared at me.

"Got it," I mumbled.

An extremely attractive girl with long legs and even longer brown hair raised her hand to ask a question.

"Yes?" the pilot said, irritated. His arms were still crossed in an X over his chest.

"Umm – what happens if we back out? You know, if we don't want to jump?"

"You don't have to jump," he said with a forced grin. "But I'm gonna keep your money because you signed this here piece of paper."

He uncrossed his arms, grabbed one of the contracts off the table and waved it in front of our faces.

"Does anyone else have any other questions before I move on?" he asked.

No one said a word.

"Wonderful. Then lets proceed."

As the ornery pilot continued with directions that made me want to run and hide in the hangar, I wondered what I was thinking all along. I was scared. This was dumb. Jumping out of an airplane wasn't going to prove anything to me except how extremely dumb I was. When the class was over we were sent to see a pleasant young man in the corner of the room who would fit us with our jump suit.

"This clips over here and – lift your arms up – yup, that's right. Okay, that's good. 'Cuz this clips over here like this. Okay! You're all set. You ready to jump?" he asked me with a big smile and extreme enthusiasm.

"No."

"Yes you are! Look at you! You look like a pro!" He turned my body toward a mirror.

"I look like an idiot."

"Well fortunately no one will see you because you'll be falling from the sky!"

"Yes, I know," I said. "Thank you for reminding me."

Outside in the hangar the rest of my family seemed excited about their jump. My 79-year-old father-in-law, Don, was pumped and ready to go.

"I've done this before, you know. About ten years ago," he told me. "I don't care if I'm 79. I'm doing it again. If George Bush can jump out of an airplane, so can I!" He laughed and patted me on the back.

I wanted to throw up. My 19-year-old niece Charle stood in her blue jumper chattering away about this, that and the other thing, appearing the least bit concerned about falling through the sky like a dead fly. She was going first. My husband stood next to her listening to her chatter away with a big smile on his face. He was grasping the buckles on his jump suit with his thumbs much like a farmer would his suspenders.

What is wrong with these people? How can they just stand there chattering and smiling? I thought their last name was Moody? They're not moody! Not in the least! They're scary! One by one, everyone in the Moody family left the hangar and jumped. And they all came back down to earth alive with big smiles.

"Are you ready, Mom?" Maddie was standing next to me, squinting her eyes in the sun to see my face.

"Not particularly, no."

"It will be fun, Mom. Just be brave. You can do anything."

My mini-Buddha.

"You next?" the grumpy pilot asked me.

"I am."

"All right. Go stand over there with Jeff and Dave. They're going to start your video and then follow you to the plane. Remember to crawl in the way I showed you."

I couldn't remember what he showed me.

"Sit tight with your feet against the back wall. When we reach ten thousand feet, you'll know what to do. See you up there."

How the hell am I gonna know what to do? I'm not gonna know. I don't know now. Would there be more instructions? My stomach moved in waves I never felt before as I meandered to the front of the hangar where my tandem instructor and photographer waited with tired smiles. I heard another instructor in the hangar say I was the twelfth jumper of the day. That meant my jump would be the twelfth time they tumbled out of a plane, one of them with someone strapped on his back.

"You ready, Joleene?" the photographer asked with as much zest as he could muster up.

I played along. "Absolutely!"

"So you're going skydiving today!" He gave me a thumbs up.

"I certainly am! And I want to dedicate this skydive to my little girl Madison-Mae who's about to watch me fall from the sky like a dead fly."

Dumb.

"All right then! Let's get this show on the road!"

We all walked toward the Cessna plane with big, plastic smiles. I hopped in, butt first, and scooted into position. Three others piled in behind me: my tandem instructor, the photographer and a girl in an orange jump suit who I have never seen before in my life. I waved weakly to Mark and Maddie and the rest of the Moody family as the plane slowly rolled out from behind the hangar onto the runway. As the aircraft picked up speed, my stomach seemed to settle down. I would be okay. Everyone else who jumped out of the plane that day was okay, right? (I would learn later that a girl I saw holding her arm and crying in the depths of the hangar had actually bumped her body hard against the edge of the plane during her jump and knocked her shoulder out of joint. True story.) I watched the sky turn from blue to white as we ascended into the clouds. Jeff made small talk with me, which calmed me a bit more.

"You nervous?" He shouted over the engine.

"Yeah," I said nodding.

"Nothing to be nervous about. It's breathtaking."

Dave the photographer nodded in agreement. The girl in the orange jump suit was gazing out the window with a smile.

"She's going to jump first. She's seasoned," Dave said.

"Okay." I turned my own gaze to the window in front of me. It was a view I didn't see very often, as it's reserved for birds and pilots and airline passengers. But it was amazing to me all the same. I felt like I was in another world. In essence, I really was.

"Put your goggles and cap back on," Jeff shouted to me over the engine. "We're hovering at ten thousand feet."

I looked at the soft rubber cap that I held in my hands. How in the world it was supposed to keep my head intact if I hit the ground with a splat was beyond me. I shrugged my shoulders and geared up quickly, situating my goggles just right and tucking my hair under the blue and black rubber cap.

"Get on your knees and scoot backward toward me, okay? I'm going to lock you in now," Jeff shouted.

Dave the photographer met me with a fist bump as I scooted into place. I could feel Jeff clipping me in.

"You're secure, okay? You ready?"

I didn't even have a chance to answer him because my breath was taken away when the side door of the Cessna flew open. Suddenly my heart stopped and my face got warm. The world below me was as little as my thumb. The wind was relentless on my cheeks. I watched as Dave hopped fearlessly onto the wing of the plane and hovered there. His camera was secure in the hat on his head. He waved to the girl in the orange jump suit to go on ahead. She grabbed the sides of the window, nodded at Jeff and simply dumped her body out of the plane. I was without words. I watched as her body got tinier and tinier as she fell through the air. At that moment everything fell silent. I was scared to death. I could feel Jeff scootching his body and mine toward the door. I could hear the young lady back in the classroom earlier asking the big question:

"Umm – what happens if we back out? You know, if we don't want to jump?"

"You don't have to jump. But I'm gonna keep your money..."

At that very moment I decided I wasn't going to go. My little girl was down there and she was my whole life. I didn't need her seeing me go "splat" all over the pavement. What kind of memory was that? I was literally inches from the edge of the plane, breathing heavily. And I was *scared – to – death.* Jeff was instructing me on what to do but I couldn't hear him. I was consumed with fear. My body was numb and my face was hot. I had, literally, three seconds to make the call. Do I stay? Or do I grow? And in that three seconds, that flash of a moment, something amazing happened. I decided to really give myself to God and leave my fate in His hands.

If I was meant to die, then that was his plan. So be it. But I had a feeling I was going to be okay. And so I crossed my arms on my chest, closed my eyes and felt Jeff push his weight against my frame. I was out the door! I could feel the wind whipping madly at my cheeks and I could hear myself going, *uhhhhhhhhhhhhhhhh!!!!!* the entire time. But I couldn't see anything because I jumped with my eyes closed. My stomach did flips and my lips turned into a smile. I was free-falling! God in Heaven have mercy, I was free-falling! I could feel Jeff's arms flailing beside me and while I wondered what he was doing, I didn't care. I trusted every move he made. Suddenly I felt a hard tap, three times, on my helmet. I thought something was going wrong so I opened my eyes and looked up. Dave the photographer was waving wildly at me in the middle of the sky with his little camera strapped to his helmet. I saw him directly in front of me, but only for a second, because the view beyond him was indeed breathtaking.

I did it.

You never saw someone smile so big as I scanned the Heavens above me and the earth below me. What I was feeling was really indescribable. It was exhilaration mixed with triumph and love and courage and excitement. I had broken through the barrier of fear and was still alive! Granted, I still had to get to the ground, but hey! I jumped, right?

In the next instant I felt my legs fly up to my nose as Jeff opened the chute. The free-fall was over and suddenly I was sailing softly through the sky. Everything was quiet.

"You want to drive?" he asked me, pushing a rope into my peripheral. I could hear him perfectly in the middle of the great big sky.

"Do I have to?" I found I was clenching the straps of my jump suit rather tightly.

"No," he laughed. "I can drive."

"Good. Because I really don't want to let go or move my arms."

He laughed again as he swiveled us to the left and then smoothly to the right. He pointed out the skyline of Buffalo, Toronto and Syracuse. I was amazed. I was still scared, but absolutely amazed. Everything I had ever feared seemed to slowly disappear as I looked around me. I felt so empowered and so alive. I was invincible, that's how I felt. And just so darn proud of myself. For the first time in a long time, I felt *awake.*

The ground grew closer as we sailed quietly toward the hangar.

"Remember to lift your legs up," Jeff said.

Of all the instructions he gave me, I got this one right. I get a kick out of watching the video because you can see my arms flailing everywhere during the free-fall as poor Jeff tries to move them into the right position. Eventually he gives up. But in this case I hit the ground fairly smoothly, and was never so happy to feel the soft green grass in my entire life.

Most people wouldn't opt to use a skydive to test-drive their fear. I still don't really know why I did. I do know it was an idea that worked well for me. It seemed to pull the fear out of my head and put it right in front of me so I could see it, taste it and touch it. I now knew what to feel and what to expect when it came to tough decisions. Nike hit the nail on the head with their *Just Do It* campaign. Because really, that's all there is to it. I would have loved to be at the table with the individual that came up with that one-liner.

Armed now with empowerment and what I felt was plenty of courage, I was able to give my employer notice that I would be leaving my job. I wasn't afraid to do it anymore. I wasn't afraid of what the next day would bring or what to expect once I was unemployed and out on my own. I put my notice in exactly one week after I jumped.

I have found this concept works well in many situations. Test-driving my fear seems to "prime" me for the big stuff. So before you do the thing that frightens you the most, do something smaller first. It should be something that still requires courage. But take it down a decibel. Cut your hair, for example. If you have long hair and have been dabbling with the idea of a short bob, why not do it? Go sit in the chair at your hairdresser's and tell her to cut it off. And as she's cutting, you'll feel the emotions moving in and out of your chest at a pace you couldn't imagine as she clips off your long locks and they slip onto the floor quietly. You'll be afraid of what you look like. You'll be afraid of what others will say. You'll also be afraid of walking into the office for the first time and dealing with people staring at you like you have five heads and twice as many noses.

If you're considering going back to school, just call your local college. That's it. Ask if you can just talk to an advisor about options. It's not like your actually going to matriculate into a program on that day, right? Just set up an hour where you can sit with someone and ask all the questions you ask yourself at night while you're lying in bed. Can I afford this? Can I work part-time on campus? Are there scholarships that can help me? Feel the fear flounder in your chest as it mixes with the excitement of a fresh, new start while the advisor shows you what your schedule might look like if you do decide to enroll. Just do a little leap before you make a big one.

Go horseback riding. Go scuba diving. Drive a hummer for the first time or hop in a hot air balloon. End a friendship or start a new one. Walk into that church instead of driving by it. Do something where the boundaries of courage aren't so harsh. *Test-drive* your fear.

If I had to breakdown the threshold of fear visually I would do it like this: imagine a plush, green parcel of land. It's wide and it's open, save a single tree not too far off in the distance. The sun is shining just right and the weather is perfect. You're standing in the middle of the grass looking at the tree. The tree is important because this is where all of your passions are. That tree is every dream, every goal, every step you've ever wanted to take to fulfill your destiny. You know the fruit of your labor hangs from this very tree and in order to continue on your way, you need to get to it. So you move forward. As you begin to walk you notice a tiny crevice in the earth at your feet. You stop and look down at it. For a second you think, *If this crevice were any bigger, it would keep me from reaching the tree.* That very thought causes the crevice to enlarge, and the next thing you know it spreads across the earth as quickly as a break in a windshield. It grows wider, too. So wide, you can't even jump over it. It's as wide as you are tall and as long as the eye can see. Now it's directly in your way, cutting you off from the tree. You can't walk around it and feel it's far too wide to jump over.

This crevice is better known as *fear*. The more you think about it, the bigger it gets. The truth of the matter is that fear is really just a tiny space between what is and what can be. As you let the fear grow, so will your doubt that you'll ever be able to overcome it.

Unfortunately, many of us will turn around and go back to where we were before. We'll leave the tree behind and it will eventually wither up and die. We won't pursue what we want strictly because of fear. Think about that. So many of us do that. We tell ourselves things to help us believe that what we want is unattainable. We let fear lead us to believe that, too. The result is an unhappy you. Do you realize that if you followed through on everything that you've ever wanted to do or try or have or see – how much happier you would be? If you would just take the chance and find your way over that tiny crevice, you would see that the fear you've built within you would dissipate in mere seconds.

Neale Donald Walsch, author of *Conversations With God* said, "I can honestly say that probably 95% of the things I was afraid of, it turned out I had no reason to be."

This is so true it isn't even funny. We put fear before us all the time. If it's foreign to us, we are afraid. If we don't know anything about it and have to take time to know it, we are afraid. If we can't see it, smell it or touch it, we are scared to death.

There are two distinct emotions felt by man: love and fear. You can't feel both simultaneously. Love is what it is. If you know someone in your life who loves you unconditionally or you love them unconditionally, you know love in the greatest capacity. If you have a pet who won't leave your side and as a result you trip over her all the time, that's love. That puppy-dog *loves* you. Fear is much different. When you feel fear, you can experience it on many levels known as sub-emotions. Anger comes from fear. Depression or anxiety comes from fear. Hate or malice also manifests from fear.

If you can just close your eyes long enough to bite the bullet and *ignore the fear*, you'll fall into that 95th percentile. You'll see that there really is nothing to be afraid of. That giant crevice in the earth before you will shrink back down into a tiny space that you only have to step over to get where you need to be. And that is all.

One more thing before I close this chapter: After I completed my skydive, I was eager to show those around me what I had done. I was so proud of myself and I just wanted to share my success with everybody. So there I was in the master control room at the news station with some of the producers and directors. They popped my DVD in and my scared little face appeared on at least six monitors in the room. They all watched a different monitor in angst, waiting for the moment when I stepped out of the plane. I watched their faces at this point. Some had their mouths open, others giggled and clapped, and one even gasped, "Oh My God, you're crazy!" But there was one director in particular who caught my eye. Without much reaction, he just watched. There was no particular expression on his face. His arms were crossed and he seemed a bit pensive, but I wasn't sure. When the video was over there was some commentary from those that had watched it, some vowing to do it someday themselves, others saying it was absolutely asinine. Eventually they all got up and headed to the break room for dinner. Except for the pensive director. He was sitting way back in his chair, arms still crossed.

"Can I ask you something?" he said, rocking back and forth in his chair.

"Yeah."

"Did it change your life?"

His question was loaded. I was amazed that someone had reflected so deeply on the very action that did, indeed, cause me to make drastic changes.

"Like you wouldn't believe," I said.

"How?" he asked me.

"Well – jumping out of that plane made me realize how brave I can really be. It also led me to where I am now."

"You mean leaving the business?"

"Yes," I said with a tear-filled smile. "It's time for me to move on."

"I want to jump out of a plane someday," he said with a laugh. "But there are other things I need to take care of first."

I didn't know what he meant at the time, but now I do. Those "other things" equated to having a child with his new wife. He's the proud Daddy of a beautiful baby girl. As far as I'm concerned, deciding to become a parent is the most courageous decision anyone can make.

When I put in my notice, it wasn't the normal two-week notice that so many give to their employers. It was a five-week notice. And that's because I wanted my last days of work to be covering the ever-popular New York State Fair in Onondaga County. Any reporter in the business reading this right now knows that when it comes to the local fair in their area, there simply must be coverage. Many dislike this general assignment. I, however, *love* it. I figured if I was going to leave the news business once and for all, it was going to be on a high note with fried ice cream, obnoxious clowns and entirely too many people in one place at one time. After one extremely brutal day in the heat, I retreated to the work truck to head back to the station. I blasted the air conditioning and stuck my face right up to one of the vents when my phone rang. It was my dear friend and fellow newshead, Tammy.

"Are you still here? At the fair?" she asked me.

"No, not really. I'm in my truck. Why? Do you need something?"

"No. I just wanted to tell you what I did today," she said with a giggle.

"Okay."

"Have you been on the midway?"

"Yes," I said. "I was just out there this afternoon. That's where the fried peanut butter and jelly sandwiches are."

"You *ate* one?" she said shocked.

"No, no. My story was on all the different fried foods they have. I was out there yapping with people about them."

"Oh," she said. "Did they say they liked them?"

"Yes, actually. But I'm not the least bit interested in trying one."

"Nor am I. Listen. Have you seen the ride out there that is kind of like a bungee jump but you sit in it?"

"No." My face was still stuffed in one of the air conditioning vents.

"Well, I went on it today," she said. "I don't do rides, but I went on this one today because I wanted to experience what you experienced when you jumped."

I pulled my face out of the vent and sat up straight.

"It's scary as hell," she continued. "I felt sick. It just shoots you straight up and you have no idea if you're going to go flying across the fairgrounds or end up safely back in place. Of course you don't really fly across the fairgrounds, but you just don't know. Ya know?"

"What happened?" I asked her. "Did anything change?"

"I don't know. I didn't think anything did. So I went back on it again. I didn't want to, but I did."

"Was this your test-drive? For something bigger?"

"Kinda," she confessed. "I just wanted you to know I tried something. It doesn't pale in comparison to jumping out of an airplane! But it was something."

"Well congratulations," I said with a big smile. "I hope it helps you overcome whatever fear you're facing."

I don't know if that little bungee ride got her to feel courageous or not, but I do know this: in the months that followed she did something pretty significant in an effort to change her life. She jumped the crevice. Even if it did have bouncy bungees attached.

Chapter 10:

Visions and affirmations.

"Dream lofty dreams, and as you dream, so shall you become. Your Vision is the promise of what you shall one day be. Your Ideal is the prophecy of what you shall at last unveil." — James Allen

To visualize a positive outcome for a particular experience that's up and coming in your life is to accept the power of the mind as being more profound than you ever could have imagined. That means you are the architect for any given experience in your life - and you get to create the outcome.

Scientists have been investigating Mental Imagery Research for decades; publishing profound studies showing the brain doesn't know the difference between real action and imagined action. Let me give you an example:

Imagine you're in the kitchen preparing a cold glass of iced tea. You want lemon to go with the tea. You head to the refrigerator and pull out a nice, fat, juicy lemon. You set it on the cutting board and slice the plump, aromatic lemon right in half. Then you pick up one half, lift it to your mouth and take a giant bite out of it.

What just happened? Did your mouth water a bit at the very thought of the extreme tartness of the lemon? The sides of my jaw are tensing up right now just thinking about it. That's because my brain can't distinguish between the real me taking a bite from the lemon - and the visualized me taking a bite from the lemon.

I used the power of visualization to prepare myself the very first time I stood in front of an audience to present a moving speech. I had presented a hundred times alone in my living room, envisioning an audience before me each time. I used the technique while lying in bed at night too. I would close my eyes and let my two very fat cats curl up around me as I imagined my presentation. I was confident as I walked on stage. The crowd would greet me with big smiles and polite applause. I would bow with gratitude before them and then begin. My words were inspiring and the audience was engaged. I was electrifying and funny and I looked smashing, by the way, because I was having a really good hair day. And when I was finished, the audience applauded wildly. I was a hit! I did this visualization every night for weeks. So when the big day finally came and I walked out on stage in front of 422 women, I was ready. I began just as I had visualized, engaging the audience within minutes. Because I placed myself on the stage in my mind so many times before, my brain couldn't really tell the difference between my visualized presentations and what I was actually delivering at that moment. My kneecaps could sure feel the difference, but I rolled through my presentation with confidence, inspiration and plenty of humor, and I looked smashing because I was having a really good hair day - just as I had imagined.

It's very possible to program your mind and body to act in ways that produce positive results. Remember the vision boards I mentioned in the last chapter? That's just one way to program your mind to remind yourself of what your passions and goals are. It's a fun project, too. I did it with my 7-year-old daughter recently. We sat together on my bed with magazines spread out before us, clipping away at pictures and words that inspired us. She was very excited, too.

"We get to cut out what we like?" she asked me.

"Yep! Cut out things you want to have or want to be. Like that dancer right there." I pointed to a ballerina. "Cut her out and paste her on the board. That way you'll see it everyday and be reminded that's what you want to be when you grow up."

"Um, Mom, I want to be a scientist, too."

"Well, then find a scientist."

"Can I cut out this cake, too? Because I would like to have this cake."

"Yes," I said smiling at her choice. "In this project you get to have your cake and eat it, too."

She didn't get it, but smiled at me all the same.

Creating a vision board is just one way to keep you moving along the path to extraordinary. What's really neat about a vision board is that you'll see your wishes reveal themselves one by one. Remember - they reveal themselves via the clock of the universe, not on *your* clock. You don't get to choose when and where your desires manifest. The Universal Spirit does. (Or God, or the Cosmos, whatever you prefer.) You don't get to decide how they come to you, either. The Universal Spirit does. The more you drill this very concept into your brain, the easier it will be to accept that *things take time.*

I put a Blackberry smartphone on my vision board. I had one issued to me when I was a reporter and I loved it. But when I left the station I had to turn it in. I was left to reactivate my old flip phone, which seemed ancient to me. Now that I was an entrepreneur, I thought a Blackberry would be an ideal tool. That little device could give me instant internet and email access, put social networking at my fingertips, provide me with a calendar, a camera, a notepad to write down ideas on the go, and a voice recorder so I could "talk out" my brainstorms.

Oh, and it's a phone, too.

Did I end up with a Blackberry? Yes I did. Here's how it happened: One summer day my husband was sitting on the edge of my father's pool following the Red Sox/Yankees game on his Blackberry. As luck would have it, he inadvertently dropped the device into the water. Completely oblivious to what happened, I watched as he dove into the pool as if he were on fire. I waited in awe for him to surface. His fist busted out of the water first, the Blackberry clenched tightly in his grip. His head followed. He mumbled a somewhat mild expletive and set his rescued phone down on the deck. He tapped it a few times, turning it this way and that to see if the screen was still functioning. I could tell by the look on his face that it was not.

"Is it dead?" I asked him from my floatie.

"Yes," he said sadly.

For the next several days he did everything he could to dry the phone out. He put it in a bag of rice. He put it on top of the dryer. He put it on top of the computer. But it refused to come back to life.

"I'm going to have to buy another one," he said unhappily.

I understood. Mark used his phone for many of the same reasons I mentioned above. It was his lifeline.

Money was tight for us, and he was reluctant to take the cash we set aside for bills to purchase one. In an effort to be frugal, he bought a refurbished Curve, the same Blackberry I had issued to me as a reporter. His original Blackberry was a Tour. And while many of the options on the Curve were the same as the Tour, it just wasn't "his" phone.

He spent several hours entering contacts, downloading applications and playing poker on the device to really make the Curve his own. And when he was done he went to the computer to retrieve the dead Tour and say good-bye.

"I don't believe this," he said walking into the living room. "My phone works!"

"We'll, that's because you just bought it," I said.

"No, not the Curve. *My* phone! The Tour! It's alive!"

I looked up to see him holding the Tour ever so happily in front of his nose. He was beaming.

"It works one hundred percent?" I asked, surprised.

"It works perfectly," he said. "Do you know what this means?"

"I get to keep the Curve?" I said clapping my hands together like a child.

"Yep!"

And so I got my Blackberry.

Now if you're wondering why I just didn't go buy it straight out like Mark did, it's because money really was tight for us. He used the cash we set aside for the electric bill to buy it. As a prosecutor he needed his email and phone at his fingertips, especially because he is often on call. So it was important he got the device. As far as the electric bill, we managed to take care of that, too. I got an extra writing gig that month that paid the bill and gave us a little extra cash to play with. The universe arranged these events in an order that got me the phone I needed and the money to pay for it – and perhaps teach my husband a lesson about cell phones and water.

You see, the universe arranges things in ways we wouldn't even think about in order to give us what we ask for. It doesn't happen the way *we think* it should happen - it just happens.

Here's another story that made me bawl because of the way it transpired:

I wanted a high-definition camera so that I could shoot my speaking presentations. I knew it was important to have myself on video so people could see what I had to offer. With my first huge conference just around the corner, I brainstormed ways to capture myself on video. I even went so far as to ask my dear friend Lacey, a former coworker, to try and get a station camera for me.

"I HAVE to shoot myself at this conference," I lamented to her. "Can't you just tell the chief photographer you need a camera for a special project and then just get it to me?"

"I'll try," she said.

I thought a station camera would be ideal because I knew exactly how to use it. If I couldn't get the camera, I wouldn't have video. And if I didn't have video, I would be devastated. Capturing video of me delivering a presentation was key for future business and the clock was ticking.

Back at SUNY-ESF, another brainstorm was brewing. I sometimes shot video for the school. Maybe I could get them to let me borrow one of their cameras? The one I was eyeballing was, ironically, the size of my Blackberry. It was a Kodak Zi8 pocket video camera and it shot in high-definition. I couldn't get them to let me take the equipment for a day, but one of the guys in the office offered to find the best deal online for me.

"It's only two hundred and sixteen dollars," Vance Blackburn said scrolling through product pages on amazon.com. Vance is the production coordinator in the communications department at SUNY-ESF, and he is the savviest online shopper I know. He loves it.

"Only?" I gasped.

"That's not bad when you consider it shoots in high-definition. Oh, look," he said, pointing at the screen, "here's a wireless microphone that's compatible with it. The microphone is only sixty dollars. Oh! Here's the tripod for the camera. Fifteen bucks. Pfft! That's dirt cheap."

I smiled weakly and walked away with a broken "Thank you" on my lips. I didn't have the money to buy all of that. It just wasn't possible, not at that time anyway. There had to be another way. I refused to do my first big conference and go home without any video.

I thought about that little Kodak camera for days. How could I get the money to buy it? What could I sell? Could I get an advance on some of my writing? Maybe I could dig up the backyard with the hopes of finding a little rusty box filled with fifty dollar bills.

Some weeks later I was driving home from SUNY-ESF, still brainstorming ways to get myself on video. If Lacey didn't come through for me, I would have nothing. But Lacey was a busy woman with a brand new baby and I knew I was asking a lot of her. As I daydreamed about someone on the street running up to my car and just handing me a camera, my phone rang. It was Lacey.

"Can you please come over before you go home? I've had a bad day and I really need a friend right now."

"Lacey, I would never tell you no, but I don't have my own car. I'm driving my father-in-law's car. Mine is up north and I have to get to the shop and pick it up before the shop closes. I'm cutting it short as it is. Talk to me now and I'll come over tomorrow."

"It can't be tomorrow," she said with desperation. "It has to be right now. Please? Five minutes. I just need five minutes."

I looked at the clock in the car. I barely had two minutes.

"Talk to me now!" I pleaded.

"Five minutes," she begged.

I couldn't leave a friend in pain. I just couldn't. Especially because I would want someone there for me in my time of need.

"Let me call the shop and see if they can leave the keys somewhere outside," I said. "I'll call you back."

"Call me back!" she repeated.

"I will. I just said I would. Let me call them and I'll call you back."

"Okay. Callthemandcallmebackloveyoubye," she slurred into one word.

I spent the next two minutes driving illegally as I searched my Blackberry Curve (wink, wink) for the number to the shop. I no sooner found it when the phone rang again. It was Mark.

"You need to go see Lacey," he said.

"What? Did she call you? How did she get your number? Oh my gosh, this must be bad."

"She needs you right now," he said in his ever-gentle voice.

"I know she does! But I have to get there before the shop closes and I left ESF early to get there on time and this is just really bad timing but I know I have to go to her because I have to go. Oh boy. I'm stressing. There's way too much stuff going on right now."

"Just take a deep breath and relax," he said. "I'll call my Dad. He and my sister can go get your car before the shop closes. You can just meet him at the house later and trade vehicles there."

He made it sound so easy.

"Okay," I said. "That's good. All right. I'll go to Lacey's right now then."

"Good. Because she needs you."

"I gathered that."

I made a left instead of a right at the next intersection and buzzed my way to Lacey's house. As I motored on down the road she texted me: *Use the front door instead of the back door. It's unlocked.*

That's odd, I thought. She never uses the front door. What's going on over there? Did something bad happen? Two minutes later I was in her driveway. Two and a half minutes later I was opening the front door. Two minutes and forty-five seconds later I was walking up three short stairs to the first landing when there, on the floor before me, was a small box. According to the details on the box, it was a rubber safety cover for a small HD camera. I raised my eyebrows. Three steps above that was a microphone. And two happy steps above the microphone was a Kodak Zi8 pocket video camera - the *exact* same one that SUNY-ESF had used, and the *exact* same one I had been thinking about. I burst into tears. By the time I reached the top step, I had a camera, a microphone, a tripod and other various accessories in my arms. And I was a blubbering mess, too.

"Why did you do this?" I asked her practically blinded by my tears of joy.

"Because you needed it and because I love you. But mostly because I never got you a wedding present and so here it is."

I was floored by her kindness. I was also blown away by the power of visualization yet again. My constant thinking about the camera set in motion a series of events that ultimately manifested the camera. I now had all the tools necessary to shoot my presentations. Lacey never knew I had been shopping around for a camera, let alone the exact one she bought for me. She was busy researching small cameras in her own little world when she decided to gift me with the gadget. The result was the Kodak Zi8.

Lots of people call this kind of activity coincidence. In a way I suppose it is. But the next time something like that happens, think about how it manifested. Have you ever bumped into someone on the street that you had been recently thinking about? Someone you hadn't seen in a long time? Nine times out of ten you say to that person, "My goodness, I was just thinking about you the other day!" Your thought patterns brought that person into your path and your visions made it a reality. Never underestimate the power of the mind. It's an amazing thing. That's why affirmations are so powerful.

Every thought you think and every word you say creates your life experience in every second of every moment. So if you choose to think "gloom and doom", that's exactly what you'll get. If you choose to think "sunshine and roses", that's exactly what you'll get. Now I want to make it very clear that this shouldn't be taken literally and that life is not perfect. This doesn't mean that not so favorable things wont happen in your life. There are always situations that will throw you for a loop. Affirmations aren't a magic trick or a hokey-pokey way out of danger or trouble. They are a way of life. The reason they work is because they are essentially a "code" as heard by our brain. Basically, your brain processes hundreds of hours of dialogue and self-talk all day. After the information is processed, you add your own conclusion. That conclusion becomes your affirmation. For example, maybe you self-talk all day about really losing weight. You consider joining a gym and buying a healthy recipe book. You talk to a friend that will join you on your crusade. You imagine how you will look after a few months. You tell yourself that it's time to finally change your lifestyle and you're ready to do it now. Once your brain processes that information, you conclude that you *can and will be successful with a healthy lifestyle.* That conclusion becomes your affirmation. You follow? Even without realizing it, you're confirming to yourself and to the energies around you that you will succeed in losing weight. When you learn to say these affirmations out loud over and over again, it makes the process even more cohesive.

Most of the time you create the conclusions or affirmations, but others can give them to you in the form of suggestion too. Throughout this book I have given you conclusions from other authors or philosophers to consider in an effort to make change. Some you'll take with you, others you won't. Regardless of how the affirmations develop, however, the more you think about them or say them, the more you will attract the very thought to yourself. So if you process information and create the conclusion in your head that you'll never find a decent job - you probably won't. If you continue to tell yourself that you won't heal and that you'll always be sick – you probably will be. If you conclude that you're overweight and always will be, then you likely always will be. Many people are unaware this process is even occurring because it's happening in our subconscious. But it's happening. Therefore, practice the art of turning your thought process around to give your brain a *new* code to work with. You'll find that things change before you that, quite frankly, will astound you. I have fought against addiction and self-loathing with this technique. I could sit here all day and tell you about it. I could even tell you I was skeptical of the power of my own mind. But I kept the affirmations up. I would imagine what I wanted over and over again and when those ideas became realities, I would think, *It's just coincidence. There really can't be a power this strong.* But time and time again, things would pop up. When I would look to the sky to say, *Thank You,* I would feel an overwhelming sense of love and appreciation.

Here are some affirmations that I use regularly:

- Maddie is safe. Mark is safe. I am safe. We are surrounded by goodness; good thoughts, good people, good circumstances.

- I am a professional speaker who is very much sought after. I get phone calls, emails and social networking messages everyday from people looking to hire me. They pay me extremely well to speak for one hour. I travel all over the United States delivering powerful, effective talks. I fly first class and stay at the finest hotels and resorts and even get free spa packages!

- I love and accept myself. I am healthy and I am beautiful. Each and every one of us is beautiful.

- I have an abundant life. Money comes easily and frequently.

I say these as often as possible. Sometimes its once a day, sometimes its twelve times a day. And I always let God or the Universal Spirit know how grateful I am for everything, too. None of this should be taken for granted. Every gift you ask for and receive should be accepted with as much gratitude as possible. Give back as much as you can. We were put on this earth to service and help others. Hold a door. Give a smile. Listen like you've never listened before. Turn it all around, right now. There is no greater feeling than the experience of change. This I promise you.

Chapter 11:

The Bridge.

"One way to get the most out of life is to look upon it as an adventure." – William Feather

To get from where you are to where you want to be takes a heck of a lot of work. It really does. Anyone who thinks it can be done with a series of shortcuts or cheats is only fooling themselves. There is no gratification in stealing money. But there is plenty of gratification when you work to make money doing something you love.

I used to visualize my miserable self sitting at the bottom of a well. Way, way above me, perhaps a hundred feet or more, was a bright light. The sun was up there. And beyond the sun was love and laughter and freedom. I could dance up there and breathe easy. I could sing and inspire and spin my little girl in circles just like they do in the movies. But I was tired. So I would just sit down at the bottom of the well and look above me. I would let my demons sit with me. All of them. And then I would get tired of who I was and what I was becoming and so I would cry, screaming and scratching at the sides of the well. Above me, a tiny hole of light showed promise. But it was *so - far - away.* I would lean against the cold, grey brick, exhausted. Then I would see the rope. The rope is always there. But I would get so caught up in finding a quick way out of the well that I would ignore the rope. But today I decide to give it a try. I grab onto the thick, coarse cord and start to pull my body up. My feet scuff along the cold, grey brick as I slowly ascend to the tiny hole above me.

Freedom.

But something happens and my mind begins to take off and I become tired again. My grip loosens and my mind doesn't want to work and so I let go.

Tomorrow. I'll do it tomorrow.

And then I fall back onto the dirt floor, defeated. I do this over and over and over again. I become exhausted. Not from the number of times I climb the rope, but from the number of times I *fall back* onto the ground. I do this for months. Those months turn into years. All the while the bright spot continues to shine above me. It never goes away. One day I can't take it anymore. I hate this life I'm living. I hate the person I've become. I don't want to live like this anymore. And so I grab onto the rope and once again I climb. I climb past my last falling point and I keep climbing. My toes clench the slimy brick as I pull my body upward toward the bright dot. I groan and scream at the pain as I climb. I want to drop back to the dirt. But I don't because I've had it. It's dark and cold and dangerous and the demons never cut me a break. All I want is the sun and I want it *now*. So I continue to pull my weight upward, ignoring the burns that are quickly developing on my hands. As I get closer to the top I begin to see more of the promise: blue skies and big, white puffy clouds. I hear laughter and I feel a sense of calmness. Maddie-Mae peeks her head into the well and smiles at me. She reaches her little hand down to help pull me out and my strength suddenly becomes that of an army. I'm almost there! I can feel the sun now. I can smell the sweetness of my child. As I reach the top I am so overwhelmed by my success that I begin to cry. My arms move up and out of the hole, touching the cool grass around the top. The sun is so warm and comforting. I feel safe as I pull my legs out and roll my back onto the grass. I'm sobbing in a way I've never sobbed before. My chest heaves up and down as the pain leaves my body and dissolves in a *poof*. Without a word my precious little girl lies down next to me. And then, "Welcome back, Mommy."

It took me years to fully emerge from that well. And when I did, I cried for weeks in waves of different emotions. Sometimes I think the tears came from me mourning the loss of the darkness that I was *so used* to living in. Other times they were tears of pain-filled joy. I was free. And I mean *free*. There were no chains to bind me and no demons around me. I kept them at bay. At first it was difficult. But I took it day by day. And then slowly, they backed away.

Even after emerging from the well I realize I'm far from done. I know I have to build a bridge to get from where I was - to where I want to be. And so I began collecting everything I needed. Sometimes I find nice, smooth planks to build my bridge with. This kind of wood is the best because it doesn't give splinters and it nails down easily. Other times the wood I build with is rotted or has holes. But I nail it down anyway, walking carefully around the rot and holes onto the next part of my bridge.

There are days I don't want to build at all. I am tired and weary, so I just sit down and look longingly across to the other side where a brilliant castle awaits me. Sometimes I lie down and disappear, but never for long. Because I remember what it was like to sit at the bottom of the well and I don't ever want to go back there. So I get up. I stand right back up and continue to look for wood to get me to the other side. There are times when friends and loved ones give me planks to nail down. Sometimes they nail them down for me. Other times, strangers give me the tools. When I'm afraid and I don't want to build anymore, an invisible power prods me a bit and shoos away the fear.

Never give up. This is your journey. Make it an adventure.

I am never alone, even when I'm standing alone. The essence and spirit of God and the Universe are with me. They are what gave me my brilliant mind and they push me to keep building. And so I do. And I am so very grateful.

Your journey will have challenges. Every journey has challenges. No one person is set aside as special enough to go through life without struggle. Your ego's voice will often make you think you are powerless over your own destiny. Ignore it. Remember: you can have, do or be anything you want. In the world of self-mastery, that's a phrase that is repeated often. I imagine that's because it can't be said any better than that. I can rearrange it or try to rephrase it, but I don't want to. I like it. And it's so damn true.

When you look at someone's life and wish it were yours, stop and think about how far you've come. Think about all that you can be. Remember that you don't know the details of the person's life you are longing to slip into. While it may look like they achieved a glorious, spectacular life without work, I'm willing to bet that is not the case. Expect to work hard. And then expect great things. Have faith and let that faith be your own. Choose to view your God or Holy Spirit or Universal Spirit in your way. This is *your* life. Mold it and build it anyway you like. The goal is to be happy. Therefore you must do what makes you happy.

Now go forth and explore your world, love your life and live with purpose.

We'll talk again soon.

My days as a television
reporter. This is from the
winter of 2007 during a
very high profile trial at the
Onondaga County Courthouse.

My mother with Madison
in 2008, a year before she
passed away. My mother
adored Maddie to pieces.

Maddie at age five making
Christmas cookies. This
smile is what kept me
motivated to heal myself.

Mr. and Mrs. Mark Moody on
our wedding day in October of
2010. I truly believe I married
the greatest guy in the world.

The big skydive! This is
just seconds after I finally
opened my eyes.

Mark, Madison and me at
the OnCenter in Syracuse to
see the musical "Wicked". I
simply adore my family.

The Kadampa Meditation Center in Glen Spey, New York.

Inside the temple. This is where the meditation sessions took place four times a day.

The "dream screen". This was taken in the dining room at the Meditation Center. Max was holding the office lamp up against it so we could see the detail.

Maddie and I at her ice skating show in March 2011.

Me at my first speaking engagement. I spoke to 422 women about overcoming fear, using the skydive video as part of my presentation.

Another speaking engagement in 2011. I also spoke to this group about fear and how to move beyond it.

Part 2:

Do Something Different

The diary of an unprepared Buddhist.

In the introduction I said I would ask you to consider doing something crazy like getting in your car and purposely getting lost so you can find your way back home. It sounds like an odd suggestion, but the truth of the matter is that doing something spontaneous or out of the ordinary can reduce the fear you have when it comes to conquering something big in your life. And yes, one simple task like driving around aimlessly until you get lost can help.

Once upon a time, in a land not so far away, I was interviewing the owner of a new business for an upcoming article. We were talking about how doing something out of the ordinary really worked in our favor when we wanted to make change.

"It's about clenching your teeth, closing your eyes and just doing it!" she said. "That's how I started my business. I just did it. I knew I was taking a chance, but failure wasn't an option, you know? It was never an option."

"I hear you," I said smiling big. "I think that sometimes it means doing something that no one would ever expect you to do, too."

"What do you mean?" she asked me.

"I mean – doing something you would never think of doing. One time, several years ago, a friend and I got into my car and we just drove. We had no agenda and didn't have to be anywhere, so we just drove. We ended up in Pennsylvania. We went to a really neat retro bar and spent the night at a nearby hotel. We were young and full of energy. It was spontaneous and it was fun."

"That makes me think of advice I gave to a client once," she said. "This woman was involved in a really abusive relationship. When she finally got out, she realized she didn't know how to do anything on her own. Her husband had always taken care of everything. I told her she needed to see that she would be just fine learning how to handle things on her own. So, I suggested she get in her car and drive until she was completely lost."

"You were suggesting she test her courage," I said smiling.

"Yes! Exactly! I told her to bring water and granola bars and all that stuff, and just get in the car and drive. Her objective was to find her way back. If she could do that – get lost and find her way back – then she could do anything."

"So did she?" I asked.

"Not right away, no. But then one day, not long ago, she called me. She was so happy and near tears that I could barely understand her. She ended up doing it! She had the whole day to herself, so she packed some things, got in her car and just drove. She was thrilled because she found her way back home all by herself."

"It's kind of metaphoric, don't you think?" I said.

"Oh, yes." She paused for a moment, reflecting on her friends joy. And then, "Other than your trip to Pennsylvania, have you ever done anything *really* out of the ordinary?"

I laughed as the image of me falling through the sky, flailing my arms like a mad woman, came to mind.

"Yes. A few times. I went skydiving recently."

"Oh!" she said with wide eyes.

"But I also did something I never would have thought about doing ordinarily. I got the idea after I read *Eat, Pray, Love* by Elizabeth Gilbert. Do you know that book?"

"Uh-huh. I know it," she said.

"Well, she kind of locks herself up in a Buddhist temple for a few months and it really changes her. So I thought I would try that. She spent time at one in Upstate New York, too. I went on the Internet trying to find which one she might have stayed at, but I had no luck. Instead I found the Kadampa Meditation Center in Glen Spey. I ended up staying there for a few weeks."

She looked at me wide-eyed.

"You stayed at a Buddhist temple? Was it amazing?"

"You have no idea," I said sitting back. "It changed me in so many ways. I was at a point in my life where I didn't know which way was up and no one in my life could show me. I needed to do something different; something completely out of the ordinary…"

And so I chose to live among the peaceful monks and nuns at the Kadampa Meditation Center for two weeks. For me the trip would do many things: for starters, it would separate me from the world I knew and I really, really needed that. Secondly, I would learn how to meditate. I believed that learning how to escape the endless chatter in my head could help bring me back to a less frenzied, more peaceful state. Lastly, it would be my recovery center. I was at a point in my life where I knew I was drinking too much. I thought if I locked myself away with a bunch of peace-loving vegans, I would be safe. And so in January of 2009, I drove four hours to the Upper Delaware River Valley having no idea what I was getting myself into or what the outcome would be. All I knew was that I needed faith - and I needed it fast.

Entry #1

January 2009

Kadampa Meditation Center - Glen Spey, N.Y.

I feel like I've been lost for a long time. A really long time. I'm not sure if I'm fortunate or unfortunate in this. Some people say that ignorance is bliss. So if I'm lost, does that make me ignorant to what is really going on around me? If so, should I be happy and revel in that? I don't know. I see so many people that seem content with their lives. They're married with a good job and have a stellar family and always appear very put together. Then again people think I'm put together. But let's be frank - if I were that well grounded I wouldn't be sitting in this little café right now, ready to write down whatever the outcome of this entire experience brings me. I wouldn't be struggling with addiction or fighting depression. I wouldn't have driven four hours to get here by myself, sucking down cigarettes, one after another, as if my very life depended on it. My bed wouldn't be stuffed in my trunk and my 5-year-old would be sitting in the back seat kicking her feet happily to the melodies of *Abba* in her little booster seat. We'd be singing out loud together and in the middle of *Man after Midnight* she would stop singing and ask me, seemingly out of nowhere, "Mommy, why do you cry all the time?"

If I really had it all together I'd be at work chasing criminals through the streets of Syracuse or knocking on the door of a parent who just lost her child in a car wreck. I'd be calling "the experts" to talk about the economy or to discuss the danger of a recently discovered wild, poisonous plant. If it was a holiday, however, I might be looking to those experts for tips on how to slim down for the New Year. And then somewhere, in the middle of it all, the scanners at the assignment desk would explode with chatter and before I could hang up the phone with the economist I just lined up for an interview, I'd be moved to *another* story where I would have to abandon the data I had already collected and jump into my news vehicle to follow the live truck to a breaking news story where a two-year old baby was found dead, apparently from being beaten to death, and left to die in her locked bedroom with just a bowl of cold chicken nuggets at her feet. If that assignment was already taken, I might be sent to the scene of a fire where four people died helplessly the night before because of faulty wiring in a rundown house, and now it's my job to knock on doors to get the morbid reaction from friends, family and neighbors.

Instead I'm sitting alone in the L-shaped café that hugs the worship portion of the temple. Ornate glass separates the two rooms. Inside the temple, a magnificent statue of Buddha Shakyamuni overlooks the now empty sanctuary, which is beautifully trimmed in gold and red. Just a short while ago I was outside in the bitter cold spreading sand along the pathways with Max from Rochester and one of the teenage boys visiting from Bethlehem, New York. Apparently doing work for Buddha earns you good merit credits? I could use a few of those. As much as the cold generally bothers me, I didn't mind standing on the back of the little Toyota truck tossing sand along the icy walkways. Physical work seems to help me forget any pain I may feel inside.

Now I'm sitting here alone waiting for the next meditation session to begin, which is kind of funny because I almost left this place. I almost threw my bed back into my trunk to drive four hours home with a Marlboro Ultra Light between my lips and a beer next to me for the drive. Yes, I almost went back to what I was. But something kept me here. And so I stayed.

Entry #2

When I arrived at the Kadampa Meditation Center I was so excited to have finally found a place where all my problems could be solved in one day. I couldn't wait for the magic to begin! I was eager to learn how to sit in the lotus position and have all my addictions and troubles disappear into thin air. How exciting! More people should consider this, I thought, as I drove the windy back roads of Pennsylvania. Perhaps there wouldn't be so much road rage.

I registered several weeks ago online for something called the Lamrim Retreat. From what I learned via the website and talking on the telephone to my very first monk *ever*, the retreat would be ideal for me. I would be studying the New Kadampa Tradition, which follows the pure tradition of Mahayana Buddhism handed down through an unbroken lineage from Buddha Shakyamuni. Lamrim, the monk explained, is a series of twenty-one meditations that teach the stages of the path to enlightenment. The retreat would cover in detail the meditations that would take me down that path. All of this in just two weeks? Wow. I imagined going back to work completely changed. People would see the difference. I would look different. I would walk different. I would smile different. I would strut around with my head held high and nothing would ever bother me. *Nothing.*

The clock in my car read 4:15 p.m. I planned on getting to the temple well in advance, but because I ended up talking to myself in the car I missed a vital turn and ended up thirty minutes out of the way. Now I was driving down an extremely windy mountain road that traced the edge of a deep, watery valley below. My driver's side window began to fog up as I peered through the glass to get a better look. I couldn't roll it down to erase the fog because the window had malfunctioned days before. If I dared touch the little black button to electronically roll it down, I faced the possibility of losing the entire window inside my driver's side door. I was disheartened when the dealer told me it would cost upwards of four hundred dollars to fix it. I didn't have that kind of money. So I decided I would have to live with it forever closed.

Through the glaze of fog I noticed that the stone wall separating the road from the deep valley below wasn't very tall. The journalist in me thought, *I wonder how many people have died going off this road?* I shook my head at the image I was conjuring. I should be thinking, *Oh my, isn't this pretty! Look at the handmade stone wall that follows this amazing road. Look at the valley below it! This is truly beautiful.* But no. Instead, I'm imagining cars flying off the road and news crews hustling to get pictures of blood and twisted metal hundreds of feet below.

The retreat started at 4:30. I had no idea what I would be walking into but I felt super-charged and I couldn't wait to get started. *Transform your life*, the website said.

"I'm ready," I said out loud. "Don't start without me!" The clock on the dash read 4:19 p.m. I really didn't want to be late. What would happen if I was, anyway? Would I get kicked out? Where do I register? Didn't the monk on the phone say something about registering inside a big, giant barn? Or beyond the barn? I couldn't remember. I was supposed to be sleeping in the barn, I knew that. Good Lord, would I be sleeping with pigs and horses? What the hell did I get myself into? In the middle of my lament I saw Sweeney Road out of the corner of my eye as I drove past it at warp speed. That's my turn! That's where I go to fix all my problems! I turned around at the next intersection and headed back up the road. Signs welcoming me to the Kadampa Buddhist Meditation Center greeted me as I turned onto the icy, gravely roadway. I leaned forward on the steering wheel to get a better look at the winter land around me. There wasn't much to see, really: icy branches, frozen ground, more icy branches. It was pretty desolate. And then a house appeared in front of me. I wondered if this was the place? I furrowed by eyebrows and I drove past it. Seconds later a parking lot with a giant barn behind it emerged on my left. *That monk wasn't kidding,* I thought. The barn was huge. I glanced again at the clock. 4:23 p.m. I didn't have time to stop and register. Not now, anyway. It was almost time. I drove slowly past the barn as four or five wild turkeys waddled across the icy roadway in front of my car. I was so intent on not squashing them, I nearly missed the great beauty that loomed before me as I looped around the barn to the main campus. Edged in brilliant gold and glowing like fire thanks to the fast setting sun, was the most amazing structure I had ever seen. It was the temple. And it opened its arms to me.

"Wow," I said out loud. I felt my heart skip a beat.

As I drove ever so slowly up the slippery road to the parking lot next to the temple, I saw a nun waddling along the walkway toward the entrance doors. She was wrapped tightly in a brown parka, her gold and maroon robes fluttering in the wintry wind beneath it. I realized at that moment that I was completely ignorant to the Buddhist tradition. Could she talk to anyone? Could I talk to her?

I found an empty parking space, slipped my car into it as quickly and carefully as possible and walked fast and light on the ice to catch up with the nun. I don't know where I was going but I was pretty sure she did. Her round little body slipped quietly through the giant doors. I slipped in just as quietly behind her. I watched as she struggled to pull a snowy boot off of her foot. Then I got the nerve to open my mouth. If she wasn't supposed to talk, I'd find out real quick.

"Is this the Lamrim retreat?" I asked the hunched over nun.

"Yeah," she said with a heavy Brooklyn accent.

Yeah?

Did she just say yeah? Nuns can say *yeah?* Really? She didn't lift her head to look at me.

I found a bench nearby and pulled off my own boots, moving slowly so I could orchestrate following her into the worship portion of the temple. I was in awe. Everywhere I turned there was an ornate statue of a different Buddha. There was one holding a sword and another holding a gem. There was one with snakes around her legs and another that was blue and closely resembled the genie from Disney's Aladdin. But I'd be darned if I was going to point that out to anybody.

The nun sat down in a chair. I chose one in the row opposite her. There were others in the temple, some sitting comfortably in chairs, others sitting cross-legged on the floor before a small, wooden table. Most of them had notebooks and pencils. I had my car keys. I was so unprepared. Suddenly there was equal movement among the mass and everyone stood. Some moved away from their seats to the wide, open aisle next to them, resting their fingertips together as they slowly bowed their heads. Was someone coming in? What are we doing? Are we praying to the statues? The blue one, maybe? Where do I look? Do I move away from my chair? *Oh no, oh no, oh no, I feel so dumb.* I must've looked pretty stupid, too. But if I did it didn't matter because nobody was paying any attention to me. They were either standing in silence with their eyes closed or looking serenely at the same door I followed the nun through just moments before. Within seconds the doors opened and a very tall, lanky man dressed in the same maroon and yellow colored robes walked slowly up the aisle toward us. He clasped his hands like the others, his head slightly bowed as his big brown eyes looked at all of us from behind his round glasses. This was Gen Kelsang. Only I didn't know it at the time. I didn't know who he was or what he was. All I knew is that everyone turned their bodies and eyes toward him as he walked up the aisle to a throne-like seat, gathering his robes comfortably around him. Soft music began playing from above. I stood there frozen, my eyes darting frantically around the temple, taking in everything as calmly as I could. Then the tall, lanky man did what I had seen on the silver screen a thousand times before; he dropped to his knees and leaned forward to place his head on the floor. My heart fell into my stomach as I watched the majority of the others follow suit. Should I be doing this too? My face was warm. Just before I passed out from sheer humiliation I noticed that not everyone was bowing on the floor. Some simply stood with their hands folded and their head slightly bowed. *Phew.* I felt the heat disappear from my cheeks.

When the music ended, everyone sat down. I followed suit. Gen Kelsang gathered his robes even closer to his body and climbed three tiny steps to the throne. He sat down slowly, smiling pleasantly at all of us and then said in the most soothing voice I have ever heard: "Hello, everyone. Welcome to the Lamrim Meditation. I am Gen Kelsang."

Not only was his voice soothing and soft as silk, it was laced with a sweet, English accent that lulled me back to ease. A giant smile crept across my face as I settled into my chair, eager to drink in everything about this place.

"This is going to be fantastic," I thought. "I'm going to absolutely *love* this."

Entry #3

"I hate this," I said to my new friend Jen. "I have no idea what I'm doing in there."

"I know, I know," she said to me from across the table. We were sitting in the kitchen of the barn, which consequently is not really a barn at all. It's a large house with dorm-like bedrooms. And while it looks like it could house horses and chickens from the outside, it's very clean and modern inside.

"I thought the meditations would be guided," I whined. "One minute I'm sitting there listening to Gen Kelsang talk about love and cherishing others and the next he leaves us to reflect on it for a whole hour! How can I reflect when I really have no idea what I'm even doing?"

"I know, right?" she agreed.

"And where do I get the book he was talking about? I don't even have a book. Or a notebook, for that matter. What are we supposed to do, anyway? Reflect, read and write?"

"I have a notebook," she said quietly.

Jennifer is from Long Island and she's got the accent to prove it. A short woman with dark hair, Jennifer greatly resembles the character Mona Lisa Vito played by Marisa Tomei in the movie *My Cousin Vinny*. Only Jennifer prefers sweats and sneakers to tight skirts and high heels.

"I don't know what to do," I said. "This isn't what I thought it would be. What's the deal with eighteen different hells and hell beings? Do Buddhists really believe that?"

"There aren't actually that many – "

"I took two weeks off of work to do this and now I don't know *what* to do," I continued. "I don't want to be here anymore. What am I supposed to tell everybody back home?"

"What do you mean?" Jen asked.

"I mean – no one knows I'm here," I said slightly embarrassed.

"Oh," she said. She didn't press me for an explanation.

"So I can't go home. Not after one day. But I can't stay here for the next two weeks pretending to meditate when I have no idea how. I'll shoot myself."

"I'm gonna go home," she said to me. "I'm not getting anything out this. I feel lost."

As did I. Now more than ever. I sighed heavily. I was holding my boots in my left hand, two fingers in each foot, and a cold cup of tea in my right. I felt no magic and no hope. And all I could think about was driving through the snow to the nearest mini-mart to get a six-pack of beer and some smokes. Forget the nuns and the monks. Forget the unguided meditation. I wanted a drink.

"I'm leaving right now," I said.

Her eyes snapped up to mine. "Right now? But it's snowing!"

"It does that here from time to time."

"Seriously," she said sitting forward. "It's a blizzard out there. Don't leave now. Leave tomorrow. Please don't drive in this."

I was tormented at that moment, but she didn't know that. She didn't know there was a storm ripping though my very soul. I could see her mouth moving as she talked, but I didn't hear her words. My mind was fixated on driving to the nearest gas station to buy what I wanted and then finding a parking lot where I could drink all by myself until the snow stopped. I would call some people, text others and likely cry the whole time. Across from me, little Long Island Jen kept talking. She didn't know why I was here. I didn't know her well enough to tell her. I knew I was in trouble when I attempted to check myself into a rehab clinic back home and the nice nurse lady told me I was a borderline alcoholic.

"I think you need thirty days inpatient," she told me scribbling those very words on a piece of paper in front of her. "Taking thirty days to heal would do wonders. I think you really need to consider it."

"While I agree with you," I said to her, "I have to tell you that it would never work. I have a five-year-old child and I don't want to risk losing her."

She stopped scribbling and looked up at me.

It's complicated," I said.

"You mean you think you would lose her if you spent thirty days here?" she asked.

"Well, yes, because I'd have to give her up for thirty days and explaining to one particular individual in my life why I suddenly need a "month-long vacation" (I did the air quotations in front of my face with my fingers) would be like putting a loaded gun to my head. I would lose her in a heartbeat."

"We'll don't you think that certain someone would appreciate the fact you're doing something about it?" she wondered.

"You don't understand," I said politely. "He doesn't know I have a problem. No one knows I have a problem."

She stared at me for a moment and then said, "Oh."

Yeah. *Oh.*

Jen moved quietly from the seat across from me to the small couch adjacent to the table. She was gnawing on her fingers, staring out the dark back door window.

"You gotta do what you gotta do," she said. "But I don't think you should leave until tomorrow."

Our conversation was interrupted when the door she was fixated on suddenly opened. A swirl of winter snow gushed around the legs of Max from Rochester as he blew in with a *'Whoo!'* Max is in his late thirties and is here for the same reason as everyone else: to find a sense of solace. I watched him pull off his snowy gloves and put them neatly on a shelf next to the door. This man has apparently been meditating since he was twelve years old. Can you imagine that? Meditating at the tender age of twelve? He's traveled the world twice over, living with indigenous tribes in tiny villages across the globe, forging a path of purpose to help instill a sense of peace in his life, and it all began when he was twelve. And he's still working on it. He unwrapped a bright red scarf covered with bits of ice from his face and neck and smiled at Jen and me.

"Hey there," he said.

"Hi Max," Jen said to him. And then quickly, "We're thinking about leaving."

I shook my head at her quick comment and buried a hand in my face.

"Why?" He pulled his knit hat off his head, moving carefully to a nearby bench to take off his snowy boots.

"I don't think this is for me," I said before Jen could speak. I was hoping he would come out with some sort of ancient Buddhist wisdom that would make me change my mind and stay, but he didn't.

"Well it's not for everyone," he replied.

"I know that," I said disheartened. "I guess I thought it would be different. I thought the meditations would be more guided."

"Haven't you ever meditated before?" he asked me, setting his snowy boots gently aside.

"No," I said curtly. "I've never done anything like this before."

"Oh," He said putting his hat on the same shelf as his gloves. "Well – maybe this isn't for you."

"I don't think that should matter," I said defensively.

"Of course not," he said quickly.

"I guess this is the part where I need a little encouragement," I said. "I'm here for reasons I'm not ready to explain and if one of you can't give me a damn good reason why I should stay, I'm going to do something really stupid and end up right back in the darkness where I was before I came here."

They both just looked at me.

I sighed heavily, wanting nothing more than to leave at that very moment. I wanted to go be with my demons. I didn't want to sit there anymore with these people. I just wanted to go home.

"You know," Jen said carefully, "you can just try and have fun with it."

I raised my eyebrows in shock. "You want me to have fun at a Buddhist temple?"

"I mean – do this *your* way," she said quickly. "Do what *you* want. You know what I mean? It's your retreat."

"Yeah," I said, having no intention whatsoever of doing what she was proposing.

"Talk to one of the nuns," Max said to me. "And you, too," he said, looking pointedly at Jen. "That's what they're here for."

141

I obviously looked unconvinced because he said again, "Or it's just not right for you."

"You know what? Let's just go to sleep and talk about this in the morning," Jen proposed. "Don't drive in this tonight. We'll leave together in the morning - *if* we decide to leave."

Now normally I do exactly what I want and I don't care what anybody else suggests. So at this point I would have stood up and said, *No thank you. I think I'm gonna leave now. Yes, I realize there is a snowstorm outside and three layers of sheer ice are covering my car. But no matter. Happy Buddha to you all. Good night.*

But I didn't leave, which amazes me because I really didn't want to stay. I think somewhere deep inside, way down deep, a teensy-weensy part of me wanted to give this a chance. I needed help and I needed it now. So I stood up begrudgingly and followed Jen to our little room where four bunk beds and a tiny little table in the corner awaited us. She crawled into her bed and I crawled into mine. We talked about love and heartache and jobs verses career. She told me about her pets and I bragged about my daughter. All the while I lay there clenching my chest where my heart is. I was hurting.

"I really need this to work for me, Jen," I said tearfully. "I took two weeks off from everything in my life to do this – to make change – and it's not working."

She lifted her head off her pillow and looked at me. Then she said something that hit me square in the forehead: "Joleene, things don't happen overnight, you know. It takes time. Whatever change you need to make you *can*. But you need to realize it takes time. Just give it a chance."

I smiled weakly at her and rolled over to go to sleep. She was right. All I had to do was give it a chance. If I didn't like it, I could leave. But I had to at least try.

Entry #4

This morning I woke up to the soft scuffle of Jen gathering her things. I lay quietly in my bunk, which was draped neatly with blankets and sheets so I could sleep privately inside. I pushed them back carefully to see her shoving one item after another in her backpack. She turned to me with a smile.

"Are you staying?" she asked rolling an orange sweater into a ball.

"I don't know," I said rubbing my eyes. "I can't decide."

She stopped stuffing and put her hands on her hips and looked at me.

"Come downstairs with me. I still have to pay before I go. You can decide while I check out."

Together we walked downstairs to the front office where a cheery nun named Suma greeted us both. Before Jen could open her mouth Suma said, "You girls are not leaving. Neither one of you. Not yet."

How did she know what we were contemplating? Oh, wait, *Max from Rochester*...

"I'm starting a new job, Suma," Jen said to her. "So I have to get home."

I stood behind her looking like an idiot.

"Not yet, you don't," Suma said.

"Well no, I don't," Jen stammered. "Not until Thursday. But I thought I would head home a day early."

"Why?" the nun asked with a smile.

Jen turned around and looked at me. I had nothing.

"I guess - " Jen sighed heavily and looked down. "I guess we feel a little lost in there. We thought the meditations would be guided."

"Well, from this point on they will be," Suma said.

"They will?" I said out loud. Suddenly, in that tiny split second, everything changed.

"Yes," Suma said cupping her hands together as she leaned on the counter. "For the rest of the retreat Gen Kelsang will be guiding each meditation. We realize there are lots of you that are new to this. So we thought it would be in everyone's best interest." Suma looked at the clock behind her. "Right now you should get ready for the first session. It starts very shortly. Tonight both of you will talk to Gen Kelsang personally. He wants to know what you think is lacking in this retreat so we can work to make things better."

Gen Kelsang? The tall, lanky, resident teacher with the smooth-as-silk English accent? The big gun? The top dog? The head honcho? The main spiritual man himself? Wow. The mere thought of being alone in his holy presence made me nervous. But okay, I'll talk to him. I decided that if this amazing being of light couldn't convince me to stay, no one could. And so Jen and I went back upstairs, got dressed and walked across the ice-cold campus to the temple where we met silence and serenity the second we walked through the great doors. There were so many friendly faces, ready to soak up the knowledge that was soon to be bestowed upon them. Within minutes we were bowing in prayer as Gen Kelsang entered the temple and made his way toward the tiny throne. He smiled at all of us and slowly opened his book.

"There are books just like this one over on that wall," he said pointing to a bookshelf off to his right. "You will need this book. If you don't have one you may get up and get it now."

I moved slowly, falling in line behind others that were without the text.

"I will guide you through each session from this point on," he said. "We will discuss four different topics each day. The stages of the path, or Lamrim in Tibetan, are a series of twenty-one meditations on the stages of the path to enlightenment. Yesterday some of you did meditations on our precious human life, death and impermanence, the danger of lower rebirth and refuge practice. Today we will discuss and meditate again on refuge practice, actions and their effects, developing renunciation for samsara and developing equanimity. Okay? So we will begin with refuge practice. Are we ready?"

Although I didn't understand half of what he was saying, I was still ready. I was thirsty for knowledge and eager to learn. I looked above me to where the top of the temple narrowed into a clean, pointed, skylight. Snow covered the glass but the bright sun pushed through it, basking us all in its comfortable, warm glow. I pulled my legs up into the lotus position in my chair and wrapped my body with a giant, black scarf I brought from home. I felt so safe at that moment. And so very grateful.

"Thank you," I whispered to the statues that sat larger than life behind Gen Kelsang. "Thank you so very much for keeping me here."

And the lesson began.

****

I learned quickly that four meditation sessions in one day were extremely exhausting. By 6 o'clock, I wanted nothing more than to crawl into my makeshift cave back in my room with my new book and a hot cup of tea. But I had to eat first. I noticed when I walked into the dining hall that there were three times as many people at the meditation center than when I arrived two days prior. Just about every table was filled with chatter and the passing of water pitchers and plates. I found Jen tucked away in the back corner eating among a group of faces I hadn't seen at the center yet. She looked up at me as if on cue and waved me over.

"Have you been to see Gen Kelsang yet?" she asked me. Her plate was full of rice, vegetables and tofu.

"No," I said, "I just walked in."

"I just came down from talking to him," she said.

"Came down? From where?"

"Up there." She pointed to a staircase that led up to a loft. "He resides up there."

"Above the kitchen?" I asked surprised.

"Buddhists are a humble people," she said smiling. "Besides, maybe he chose that room because he gets hungry at night."

"So what did you talk about?" I asked her.

"That's private," she said sheepishly. "But I did thank him for guiding the meditations. I think it's really helpful. Don't you?"

"Oh, absolutely. But I'm exhausted."

"It can be mentally draining, all that visualization and reflecting. Sometimes I fall asleep," she confessed.

"Is that bad?" I asked, wide-eyed.

"We'll I don't think I'm the only one. Meditation takes practice. I wake up the second someone sneezes. And I'm never gone for very long. You should eat and then go talk to him. He's waiting for you."

I nodded and got up for a bowl of hot soup and buttered rice. No meat. I ate quickly, eager to get my talk over with. I was really nervous. But I didn't tell Jen that. By the time I finished eating, the majority of guests had cleared out. Some still lingered at their tables, talking softly with their new sangha friends about the day's lessons.

I brought my plate into the kitchen where a very tall, bald man took it out of my hands. He was wearing a red flannel shirt and jeans and appeared very down to earth. I could tell immediately that he was a kindred spirit.

"I'll take your plate, then," he said with a big smile. He, too, had an English accent.

"Thank you," I said.

"Are you enjoying the retreat?" he looked up from the tub of suds to me.

"Oh, yes. It's – different."

"It's lovely, don't you think?" He was still smiling.

"I don't know if it's exactly lovely, but it's nice."

"I'm Dave," he said, drying his large hands off on a towel above his head. He extended the right one to me for a handshake. "I was the one driving the truck while you helped sand the grounds yesterday. Thank you for your help, chicken."

"Chicken?" I said a bit stunned.

"It's a term of endearment," he said with a big smile.

"Oh!" I laughed out loud. "Well, hello to you, then. I'm Joleene," I said accepting his hand.

"Joleene! Isn't that a pretty name. Isn't there a song out there with your name in it?"

"Yes. And I've never heard it before," I said playing into his joke.

"Well then, I best not sing it to you!" He laughed again as he plunged his hands back into the water to finish the task of cleaning each plate, one by one.

"I have to go see Gen Kelsang," I told him, shoving my hands into the back pockets of my jeans. I don't know why I felt compelled to tell him that, but I did.

"Oh, really? You're going up to talk to the boss, are ya?"

"I am." I looked down at my feet. "And I'm a bit nervous about it."

"Don't be," he said. "He is the same as you and I, believe me. One of these days I'll have to tell you the story of how I met him when I was in England. You should come by some evening and well chat over tea. In the meantime, you best go see him now. Don't want to keep him waiting."

I nodded in agreement and left the large man in the red flannel shirt to finish cleaning up. I walked slowly up the staircase to the top of the loft where two doors awaited me. I was afraid to knock, God only knows why. But I didn't have to. A nun came up behind me and opened the door for me, showing me which way to go with by direction of her hand. I nodded politely and moved into a quaint room where I sat down in a chair across from Gen Kelsang. He was sipping loudly from a soup bowl. The nun waved at me with a smile and closed the door behind us.

It was an awkward moment, to say the least. I mean, imagine this: on one side of the room there's an ordained spiritual teacher (whom I would later learn is renowned and highly regarded in the streets of England), honored with the opportunity to be the resident teacher at Kadampa in New York, sipping out of a soup bowl. On the other side of the room, there is a somewhat ordinary 36-year-old woman who's *never* practiced Buddhism in her entire life, and is about to give the resident teacher input on *his* retreat. I sat stiff as a board in my little chair as he finished up the last of his meal. He looked up at me from behind the bowl as he gulped. Then he set it down on the dresser next to him and folded his hands in his lap.

"Okay," he said gently. "How are you?"

I just stared at him.

"You prefer the guided meditations?" he asked.

I managed to nod.

"Have you ever meditated before?" He smiled at me now.

"No," I squeaked out. "But I've listened to Eckart Tolle and I've tried meditating with him. It doesn't last very long. But (big sigh) - I'm actually here for a different reason."

He nodded.

"I'm here because I'm struggling with (my mouth went dry) - addiction. I'm trying to use the meditation center as my place of recovery."

He raised his eyebrows and reached for his cup of tea without taking his eyes off of me.

"Addiction? What kind of addiction?"

Oh boy. He's gonna kick me out.

"Umm, well cigarettes, for starters," I said.

"Mmm-hmmm," he said sipping the tea.

My knees were shaking now. Suddenly there were so many things I wanted to tell him but I didn't know how.

"And alcohol," I managed.

He looked at me for a long while and I thought that maybe he had nothing to say. He sipped his tea once more, never taking his eyes off of me.

"You're an alcoholic?" he asked gently.

"Well, no, I don't think so. But I'm close. I don't wake up craving the stuff, but I don't turn it away when it's offered, either. Someone told me recently I was a borderline alcoholic. I have a tendency to binge on lots of things, not just alcohol. Apparently I have an addictive personality."

"I see," he said.

"So I made the choice to come here to try and heal myself. Elizabeth Gilbert went to a temple in the book *Eat, Pray, Love* and I thought maybe I could do something like that, too. But she didn't have an addiction. At least not that I'm aware of, anyway."

He had no idea what I was talking about.

"Do any of these meditations over the next two weeks address addiction?" I asked quietly, as if my demons were listening. "I mean, it's suffering, isn't it?"

I was hoping he would say, *Why yes, Joleene, our next session covers addiction completely. Not to worry. You will be saved and life will be harmonious from this point forward.*

But he didn't. What he did say however, was just as good.

"It is suffering, yes. Absolutely. It's part of Samsara. (Samsara is the indefinitely repeated cycles of birth, misery and death caused by karma.) Your making the decision to come here to heal is wonderful. It's wonderful and yes, it can work for you, if you let it. Pain is inevitable," he said. "But suffering is optional. Do you understand what that means?"

"I think so."

"It means you don't have to use your bad thoughts to suffer. You can change them. We all feel pain on some level at some point in our lives. It's how we handle it that makes all the difference. If we dwell in the pain, then we suffer in the pain. But if we learn to break free from it, then we don't suffer. Do you see?"

"Yes," I said, feeling a bit lighter.

He smiled at me like the proud teacher of a student that just discovered two plus two does indeed equal four.

"But it takes work to become free of suffering," he continued.

I nodded.

"It's like starting a new job," he said. "When you first start the job you're just - okay at it. That's because you've still got a lot to learn, right? And so you go back every day to learn. You also go back because you need the paycheck. That's your reward at the end of the week for learning the job, the paycheck. And so every day you go back, and every day you get better. Soon the job becomes second nature. Soon, for you, practicing love and patience with yourself and others and learning to do for others will *also* become second nature. Then the paycheck for you - will be the joy and happiness you feel inside because you have succeeded. No more suffering. You understand?"

I did understand and it made me smile. It takes work to change. I knew that. I've always known that. But for whatever reason it didn't hit home until Jen reminded me the night before. Now it was really sinking in. I knew I could no longer go on feeling the way I was feeling and doing what I was doing. Now, sitting in front of Gen Kelsang in a tiny room above the kitchen somewhere in the depths of the beautiful Upper Delaware River Valley, it just felt right. At that very moment, I made a vow: I would stick out the two weeks at the temple and work as hard as I possibly could to straighten out my life. I had to. I would make it work. I would ask a hundred questions and teach my mind to be still and learn patience and turn it all around. I had all the tools in front of me. I was a fool to do anything else.

"I understand we have lots of new people here at the retreat who could use some guidance in the sessions," Gen Kelsang said. "So I will be guiding all four sessions everyday for the rest of the retreat. Do you think that will help?" He smiled and nodded at me as if to say: *This is the part where you agree with me, okay?*

"Yes, it will help," I said. "And I am so very grateful. Thank you."

He nodded again and I stood to leave. I glanced at him one last time before I left the little room. Downstairs it was quiet, save one table in the corner where Jen was sitting with Dave from England. As I descended the loft stairs, they both turned to look at me.

"Are you staying?" she asked me.

"Oh yes," I said beaming, my heart felt full. "I'm staying."

Entry #5

Over the past few days I've paid close attention to the teachings and have worked very hard to push any negative thoughts out of my mind while I'm meditating. I arrive at every session on time and sit in the same seat. Once I'm settled in my chair, I pull my legs up into the lotus position and wrap my giant, black scarf around me to keep warm. Then I pull out my notebook and pen and wait eagerly for Gen Kelsang to arrive. And when he does I hang on every word.

I feel so comfortable and warm in my little chair inside the temple. I'm slowly learning to fall into the world of guided meditation. Every day we learn a new teaching and then meditate on it for twenty-five minutes. This is the fifth day of the retreat and I couldn't wait to curl up in my chair to learn something new today. On this particular day I was taken off guard, however. Gen Kelsang announced we would be meditating on the advantages of cherishing others. And as I do *so* very well, I cried uncontrollably through the entire teaching. Tears rolled down both cheeks as I sat in my chair, listening intently to his words, ignoring the snot that ran out of my left nostril.

Gen Kelsang sat before us on the small throne with his eyes closed and said, "Picture your friends and your family sitting all around you. Maybe you're at a park, maybe you're at home. Just put them all of them in one place. Okay. Now one by one, tell them how much you love them and cherish them. Let them know what they mean to you. Tell them how much you appreciate who they are. Tell them everything. Close your eyes now. Begin. Start with someone that you really, really cherish and just tell them how you feel."

Immediately Madison-Mae came to mind. She was sitting on the living room floor of our apartment with her knobby little knees pulled up to her chest. She was smiling real big at me. That's when the tears began. Nary a word came out of my mouth and the water works came on full force. My heart felt full and I dropped my pen in my lap to cover my chest with my hands. I love that little girl with everything I have. Suddenly all of the pain I had caused myself through self-loathing and beating me up over the years came gushing out. I felt guilty for feeling such pain. I should have been more focused on my child. Instead I was too busy hating myself and everyone else around me.

"I cherish you," I whispered out loud to my little girl. "There is nothing I wouldn't do for you. Nothing. You are my world."

She smiled at me and rocked back and forth on her bottom, clenching her knees to her chest. Behind her, other family members were slowly beginning to emerge. Next to her was my former beau; one I had let go of so that I could find my way back to a healthy, safe place in my life. He stood up, taking Maddie's hand as she stood up with him.

"I cherish and appreciate everything about you, too," I said to him. In my mind I took his hand and looked into his eyes. My heart exploded at that moment. I felt so much appreciation for his patience with me and I loved him for that. But I was pained at the same time because I had caused *him* so much pain.

"I'm so sorry," I said to him. "So very sorry."

"Mommy, don't cry," Maddie said to me. I turned to her and knelt down before her.

"I love you like you wouldn't believe, little girl," I told her. "You are *everything* to me. Without you and your spunky style I wouldn't be here right now. And it's *good* that I'm here. So just sit tight, baby. I'll be home soon, okay? I love you."

"Where are you?" she asked me.

"I'm someplace safe."

"Okay, Mommy. I love you, too."

I turned away from both of them to find myself standing in my father's kitchen. He was sitting at the breakfast bar, just beaming at me.

"Hi Dad."

"Hi, Jo!" he said happily.

"I love you, Dad. And I cherish you. I know we've both made some mistakes in the past and there's been an awful lot of anger between us. But I always love you."

"I'm not proud of those mistakes," he said to me, looking down.

"Nor am I, Pop. But no matter what, I love you."

"I love you too, buddy Jo," he said to me.

Next to him his wife was smiling at me.

"I cherish you, too," I said to her. "Thank you for all the good eats and allowing me to stay in your home when I was down. I really appreciate that."

She nodded at me, still smiling.

I wanted to say more, but I thought it best to leave it just as it was. I turned away from them both to see my mother standing before me. I was back in my living room now. She stood there with her arms crossed, a slight smirk on her face. This was the woman who brought me into this world. She loved me and kissed me and scolded me and spanked me, raising me the best way she knew how. But somewhere along the line we fell apart. She could never really look me in the eye, especially when I told her that I loved her. Now, even in my meditation, she couldn't find my focus.

"Mom. I cherish you, you know. More than you realize. I may not show it all the time, but it's true. You've done so much for me, especially these past few years. I'm grateful for that. I will work harder to accept you as you are and love you no matter what."

She just stared at me, not responding. Her husband stood behind her. I took a deep breath in my meditative position, adjusting my legs in the chair. It was perfectly quiet inside the temple and I was still and unalarmed until a large ball of ice rolled off the glass roof above me and crashed loudly to the ground below. I opened my eyes and looked around the sanctuary. No one else seemed to notice. I closed my eyes again to find my mothers husband still standing before me.

"Hi," I managed to say. He just looked at me with a quiet grin, waiting for me to say something to him. I struggled for a moment. I didn't know what to say. My connection with him was weak. I was about to turn away from his eyes but I couldn't. I had to find what I cherished about him. I looked at my mother who still had her arms crossed. She wasn't really grinning anymore. I knew she wanted me to say something. And so I took a deep breath inward and managed, "Thanks for taking care of my Mom."

He nodded, still with a strange grin on his face, and stepped back to allow my big brother to move forward.

"Hi, Jo," my brother said.

"Oh, hey Sean."

"What is it like there?" he asked curiously.

"It's quiet. Reflective. Very helpful to me."

"Yeah?"

"Yeah. I think you would like it here," I said. "But we can talk about that later. Right now it's time for me to tell you how much I appreciate you."

"I figured that. Look, I know I don't come around much," he said, "I guess I like to keep to myself."

"That's okay. I can still tell you what you mean to me and thank you for all the laughs. We'll always have that," I offered.

"True."

"So just be good to yourself and know that I love you no matter what. I'm trying to make progress here. I don't know why I was drawn to this place but it just feels right. I'm happy. I could stay here forever."

"Really?" he asked with the same piqued curiosity.

"Oh yes! There is no drama here. Just serenity. So many wonderful people, too. This is what living is all about…just accepting what is and loving those around us."

"You make it sound so easy," he said.

"I know. I do. But it takes work. I still have a long way to go."

He nodded and said, " I love you, Jo."

"I love you too."

And then they were gone. All of them. I stood there alone, my heart surging with the pain of the emptiness of the room. I turned around to face my kitchen, only to find myself standing in the middle of the newsroom. It was moving at its normal steady pace: not too fast and not too loud – just moving with regular everyday news sounds and motions. I stood by my desk quietly watching the organized chaos. An engineer zipped past me and glanced up for a quick, "Hello." The scanners at the desk buzzed with the possibility of a car accident as the assignment editors fielded telephone calls from concerned drivers. Lacey, my dear friend and the station's traffic reporter, zipped past me to scoop several pages off the printer behind me. She was the only one I ever really shared any of my suffering with. She is a wonderful friend and I love her to pieces.

"Lacey," I asked as she gathered the pages off the printer, "do you have a minute?"

"A minute is all I ever have around here!" she answered with a big smile. "What's up?"

"I need to talk to you."

"Uh-huh?" she buzzed past me again with the freshly printed pages clutched tightly in her grip, waving at me with her right hand to follow her back into the traffic studio. Her fast-paced gait told me she had to be in front of the camera in just seconds. I followed her into the tiny studio and closed the door behind us. She tossed the papers onto her desk, turned her lavaliere microphone on and stepped in front of the camera just in the nick of time.

"*Goooood* afternoon, Syracuse! It's twenty-two minutes past four o'clock. I'm Lacey Johnson with a live look at your outbound drive time. Interstate 690 is a wreck right now because of a minor crash and there are some delays due to rubber-neckers eastbound. Use an alternate route or pack your patience as you travel 690 this afternoon. Miles of smiles east and west bound on the New York State thruway! Slow it down a bit, folks. I'll be back live in fifteen minutes."

She turned her microphone off, swooped quickly into her chair, looked up at me with her big brown eyes and then rolled herself snugly up to her desk.

"What's up?" she asked me in her lovely, southern drawl. "How *are* you?"

"I am well," I said as she grabbed both my hands.

"How you doin' there?"

"Good, good," I said. "Staying out of trouble."

"Yeah?"

"Yeah. Ummm - I came back real quick just to tell you that I really do cherish you. I cherish you and love you and appreciate all the time you've ever given me in this tiny little room. Our talks have helped me so much and I can't thank you enough for that."

She clenched both my hands and whispered, "Your welcome."

"If there's ever anything I can do for you, I will, Lacey."

"I know that, honey," she said.

"I gotta go now."

"All right," she said with smiling eyes. "Come back to work quick, though, okay? I'm lonesome here without you."

"Okay," I said. She hugged me tight and winked at me as I walked out the door.

I stood in the open hallway and took a deep breath. My dear friend and co-worker Tammy was walking quickly toward me with her head down, attempting to balance two very large bags on her right arm while carrying an awkward sized make-up box in her left. I had a feeling the box was going to bust open at any moment, covering the floor before us with shimmery shades of blue, red and gold eye shadows.

"Do you need a hand?" I offered as she used her knees to stop the box from tumbling to the ground.

"No, I think I've got it." She adjusted the bags to balance herself. The box hit the floor anyway. Thankfully, it didn't bust open.

"I think you need to downsize your make-up selection, don't you?"

She laughed as she reached for the box.

"Aren't you supposed to be gone?" she asked me, finally looking up.

"I am gone. I just stopped in to chat with some folks."

"Oh," she said. "About what?"

"About how much I cherish them. What they mean to me, what you mean to me, stuff like that," I said.

"Uh-huh."

"We've known each other nearly ten years," I said to her, "and I love our conversations and our little dinners out. I wish you were still working in Syracuse so you were closer."

"How convenient that I'm here right now for this chat then, eh?" she said laughing.

"Well that's the beauty of imagination. I get to pick out the people I need to address. You were one of them. That's because you are so authentic. I love that. You're so very good at what you do, too. You taught me so much. You lent me your knowledge as a reporter and had me walking away from every situation thinking, 'What would Tammy do?'"

She laughed, finally finding a good balance with everything she was carrying.

"Well at least I'm good for something," she said smiling.

"You're good for a lot of somethings," I told her. "Let me hug you. Just stay where you are and don't move or you'll lose everything."

She laughed out loud again as I maneuvered my way into her arms.

"I'll see you soon," she said. "Well do dinner. Indian next time."

"You got it."

And she hobbled away down the hall with her life in two bags and a box.

Alone in the hallway, I saw my supervisors' door was right in front of me. It stood there, wide open, yet I hesitated going in. I reflected on the number of times I sat in that office, not because I was being reprimanded, but because life would throw me curve balls that I just didn't know how to hit and I would have to wander into his office and explain myself, often with my head down in shame. I hated that my life was so "messy" and troublesome. But more than that, I hated that I had to reveal so many parts of it to him. There were days I had to go in and tell him I had to leave early or not be there at all because of child custody issues. It was humiliating. After that period of my life subsided, I had to go to him again because of problems I was having with a fellow employee. And just when he thought the smoke was finally clearing in my crazy little world, I ended up in his office *again*, this time with my latest demon strapped tightly to my back, barred down with huge locks and rusty chains. In order to slay the demon, I told him I needed two weeks off. He gave it to me.

I watched him through the glass for a moment. He was eating his lunch, squinting hard at something of interest on his computer monitor. Conjuring up some nerve, I tapped quietly on the open door.

"Hey there," I said, walking in.

"Hey, Joleene!" he said in a cheery voice.

"I just wanted to tell you how much I really appreciate everything you've ever done for me. I know it's been crazy sometimes. But you need to know that it doesn't go unnoticed and that I genuinely cherish you."

He stopped chewing and stared at me blankly. Inside the temple I started to cry. It was so difficult for me to express myself to this man. I was quite certain he already thought I was a nut job. Nothing like adding insult to injury by throwing the ol', "I cherish you" line his way. My heart twisted with pain as I cried at my own humility. There was so much I wished hadn't happened – so much I was embarrassed about. In my heart I believed I was nothing but a problem to this man. He was the one who gave me my job and I was sure he regretted it because of the drama I was constantly bringing into his office: my personal fight for my daughter, an issue with a coworker that involved human resources, a physical attack on me that limited my ability to carry my gear, and now a two-week leave of absence so that I could get my shit together. Imagine his surprise when he learned I took off to do it at a Buddhist temple.

I closed my eyes and was back in his office. He was still staring blankly at me.

"What's that?" he said holding his sandwich perfectly still in front of him.

"I said I cherish you. I appreciate all you have done for me. It's because of you that I'm able to be here."

"Yes, well – where are you again?"

"In a good place," I said with a smirk. "I just wanted to take a minute to let you know that I'm working very hard to pull out of this. I'm so humiliated right now. I never expected all of this – stuff – to ever happen. So I wanted you to know that your patience is truly appreciated. You have to know that."

A dollop of tuna fell out of his sandwich and hit the wax paper below it. He didn't notice.

"Well thank you," he said perplexed.

"Sure thing." I stood there awkwardly.

"Is that it?" he asked.

"Oh, yes. That's all."

"Great," he said with a smile. "Can you close the door behind you when you leave?"

"Sure thing," I said again. And I left.

I wandered back into the hallway and took another deep breath. I wasn't quite done talking to the management team. The door immediately next to my supervisor's was the assistant supervisor. I watched as he pecked away at the keyboard, working feverishly with his head down to finish a story for the 12 o'clock news. I knocked gently on the door jam.

"Can I come in?" I asked him.

"Sure," he said without looking up. "Do you need me to copy edit your story?"

"Uh, no. I'm not at work."

He stopped typing and looked at me in the doorway.

"But you're standing right in front of me."

"Yes, but I'm not really here. I'm actually a few hundred miles away right now. I just stopped by to say something to you."

He looked guilty.

"What did I do?" he asked me.

I laughed out loud and crossed my arms as I leaned into the doorway.

"You didn't do anything. I just wanted to let you know that I am sorry for all the times I gave you crap. I do it a lot, I know. But I truly cherish who you are. That's all. You have great patience for me and I really appreciate that."

"You what?"

"I cherish you. I appreciate you," I repeated.

He laughed out loud and went back to his pecking.

"I cherish you too, Joleene. Now go away!"

The sound of a gentle gong inside his office morphed me back to the interior of the temple. It was time to wrap up our meditation. I moved from the doorway down the hall toward the exit. But not before bumping into the senior reporter. He raised a Styrofoam cup of coffee into the air to keep it from spilling on his jacket as I buzzed past him.

"Whoa, Miss Thing! Where are you going in such a hurry?" he asked circling around me.

"I gotta get back. The bell rang. But I'm glad I bumped into you! Because I wanted to let you know that I genuinely appreciate who you are. Even if you do have a morbid sense of humor." I winked at him.

"What the hell are you talking about?" he asked me. He was still holding his coffee above his head.

"I think you're awesome, okay? I respect you highly. But you already know that. What you *don't* know is that I cherish you. I hold you in high regard."

"Cherish?" he said furrowing his eyebrows.

"Yes. In other words, I hold you dear. I appreciate you."

"I know what the definition of the word is, thank you very much. I'm just trying to figure out why the hell you're telling me this."

"Because that's what I'm doing right now," I said.

"I see," he said, finally lowering his cup. "Well – then I cherish you, too. And I cherish the next person that walks past me."

"That sounds fantastic," I said. "Although something tells me you don't mean a word of it. Take care, okay? I'll see you in a few weeks."

We went our separate ways, me heading back to my seat in the temple and him heading back to the newsroom shaking his head at me, going on still about whom he promised to cherish.

The gentle gong sounded again. I took a deep breath and opened my eyes. I was tired. Gen Kelsang was sitting perfectly still in his seat, his eyes closed. I held my breath for fear of disturbing anyone else that was still coming out of his or her meditation. It was so still and peaceful inside the temple. I felt warm and safe wrapped in my big, black scarf. Not even the wind and ice outside could take that away from me.

I looked around at some of the others I had gotten to know since my adventure began at Kadampa. Three seats away from me in the same row was Kay, a private girl that had no interest in giving out any information about who she was or where she came from. In the front of the room were four spunky teens from Bethlehem, New York. Not far from them was Kevin from New York City, Sara the singer and a cheery girl named Maria. I cherished all of these people, too, for allowing me to share space with them as I ventured into the depths of my soul, pulling out some incredibly deep-seated feelings that I never knew existed.

But how did those feelings gain such momentum? How was it I was able to dig down so very deep and pull them up and out of me? *Cherishing* someone? Never before had the word even entered my vocabulary. I didn't really cherish anybody but myself. Yet in my head I had just wandered through my living room and my place of employment, stopping to chat with those that I genuinely cared about, just to tell them what they meant to me. Suddenly I wanted to know everything that was happening in the world. I wanted to know about my friends and their hurt and I wanted to know about complete strangers and their hurt. Before my stay at Kadampa, any news story I read or heard that affected people outside a fifty mile radius of me seemed like a dream. They were only stories. It was like the situation didn't really exist except in a news clip. Now I realized I was part of a much bigger picture. Yes, I was that consumed with self-pity and self-loathing that I had closed off the entire world around me. Now years of stifled compassion was beginning to surface in response to everything I'd ever ignored. It was flowing out of me like crazy.

"Are you okay?" Sara the singer asked me. She sat down next to me, her face drawn with concern. The temple was empty now, save the brilliant statues that watched cautiously over us.

"Gosh, I hope so. I can't stop crying. That session was so powerful. Wow." I looked up at her. "Does this happen to you? Do you cry the entire time your meditating? I must be doing something wrong."

"Oh, no!" she said. "You're not doing anything wrong! Are you kidding me? As a matter of fact, I envy you. I wish that happened to me when I meditated."

"You wish you cried? Really?" I turned in my chair to face her now. "It's not much fun. Especially when your nose runs as much as mine."

"Well, you must be pulling up some pretty deep feelings to be in this condition," she said.

"I just realized so much during this last teaching. There is so much I am missing because I'm not giving to others. I've been selfish."

"Oh, honey, we're all selfish from time to time," she said. "We live is a society that teaches us that. The beauty is that people like you and I work hard to *not* be selfish."

"But how do I practice not being selfish?" I asked her.

"Just keep loving. Most importantly, however, learn to love yourself first."

"Wow. Well, I haven't the foggiest idea how to do that," I said.

"You're doing it right now," she said, gently touching my arm. "Welcome to the beginning of change."

Entry #6

There are many outdoor pathways that make up the landscape of the Kadampa Meditation Center. I've ventured a few on my own but today I chose to walk with Kevin from New York. He's heading back to the city, but not before he attempts to teach me how to live in the present moment, which in this case, is outside in the freezing cold.

"You just have to let everything in your mind dissolve. Know what I mean?" He skipped carefully atop a few rocks in an effort to get over the fast flowing stream where the forest path began. "I listen to the crunch of the snow with each footstep," he said as he turned around to watch me do the same. I was already frozen to the bone. "I take in every sound and every breath and I just walk. I don't let any other thoughts filter through."

"Like the thought that I'm freezing out here," I said sarcastically.

"Exactly!" he said excitedly. "That's perfect! You know you're cold but you have to ignore it. Nothing else should exist. No work, no stress, no worries. Just the moment you're in. You know? Don't think about anything else because you don't need to."

"Okay," I said, standing at the edge of the forest with him. "But just for the record, the moment I'm in includes the freezing cold. So aside from that, I just – take in what's around me?"

"Yes. Don't think of anything else except what you see. This is the only moment you have. *Live* in it. Revel in it. Don't go backward to work or forward to tomorrow. Stay right here where you are."

I've walked a thousand miles down a dozen roads in a handful of different ways: trudging up this hill, strolling down that path, meandering across fields and over railroad tracks, and not once did I ever stop to take a good hard look at what was around me. I remember several years ago my father saying to me, "Jo. You gotta slow down. Stop and smell the roses." I didn't know what that meant at the time and I took it literally. There I was, walking down the railroad tracks behind his house one day when I saw a group of yellow flowers smiling at me. So I stepped of the rusted tracks, plucked one of the flowers from the earth, brought it slowly to my nose and smelled it. Nothing. No smell. So I tossed the flower to the ground and thought: *There. I did it. I stopped, slowed down and smelled a flower. Happy?*

But I never actually *slowed* down. Not until now.

I walked quietly along the icy pathway, listening carefully to every sound around me. From the crunch of the sparkling, white snow below my feet to the trickling water that rushed between the rocks and sticks in the tiny stream below a small wooden bridge, I listened. I even stopped and watched the water move over the rocks as if I had never seen water before. I don't know what Kevin wanted me to find in that noise, but I opened my mind and listened all the same. When the wind blew I looked up to watch it rock the top of the trees to create, quite frankly, one of the most beautiful sounds I think I have ever heard. Every tree was glazed with ice and every branch heavy with its glisten. I do not exaggerate not when I say it created a symphony that melted my soul. Then, only for a moment, the chatter in my brain disappeared: My ever-running to do list, the turmoil I felt regarding my last failed relationship and the strained connection I had with my mother dissolved as I looked to the top of the trees for a better view of the icy musicians.

Is this what my father was talking about when he told me to stop and smell the roses? All of this beauty? Is this what I've been walking past all my life? Kevin stopped in front of me to look toward the sky. He, too, heard the symphony among the trees. We looked at each other and smiled. I suddenly felt the same warm comfort I experienced the day before in the temple. For an instant I was living in the present moment. There was no fear and no worry. There was no guilt and no shame. There was only what is. And what is, is beautiful.

We moved onward, really looking for unique things among the trees. Kevin spotted a frozen clump of red leaves on a bush while I marveled at a glittery pile of twigs on the ground.

"Look at this," he said pointing to a white bubble next to the motionless red leaves. "It's a frozen cocoon of spiders."

"Oh wow. It's pretty neat looking," I said.

Through the thin glaze of icy water that molded the cocoon into perfect shape were hundreds of tiny spiders, forever suspended in time. They would never know what tomorrow would bring.

"Poor fellas never got to explore their world," he said closely inspecting his find.

"Now *that's* living in the moment!" I joked.

"I suppose it is," he said with a grin.

We trudged on, breaking fresh snow on a different path that led up a hill to an open field. Here the trees were stripped of their bark.

"Hungry deer," he says pointing at the trees. "As quiet as it is out here, we're never really alone."

"Nope."

"You know," he said looking outward over the field, "I walk this trail every morning by myself. I come out nice and early so I can walk alone. But when I came out yesterday I was halfway through my walk when I discovered a set of footprints. At first I was a little disappointed because I didn't feel like running into anybody else, you know? I just wanted to be alone. I admit it was self-cherishing but I guess I was content being out here in the silence. So for the hell of it I followed the footprints to see where they led. And you know what I discovered?"

"What?"

"That they were my own."

"So you really were alone," I said.

"Yeah, but *not* really. I realized that even when we're dwelling in the darkest and most desolate moments in the dreariest corners of our minds, we're never really flying solo, you know? I think somebody somewhere wanted me to realize that, so they sent me on a path to follow my own footsteps."

"You see the magic in everything, don't you?" I asked him.

"I guess I do. But that's the beauty of living in the moment. There are no mistakes. Everything happens for a reason and that's the truth. Some of the things we go through happen so we can learn patience and compassion. Sometimes silly little things, like following your own footsteps, can teach you something. No matter what it is, those instances uncover the real you."

I nodded in agreement.

"So now what?" I asked him.

"Now we follow our own footsteps back to the temple for some warm tea."

I nodded again and followed him back along the twisty, icy trail to the temple. Warm was good. Wisdom was good. And being with such a compassionate person was good. I have some wonderful footsteps to follow.

Entry #7

I must admit that I am an expert when it comes to crying. I'm pretty sure I'm a natural. I can't remember the last time I cried *so much*. I think I've been crying for seven consecutive days now and I'm still not done. Just when I thought everything was okay and I was on top of the world, I fell off the top and crashed and burned.

It started last night with a very strange dream. Lots of my dreams are strange, but this one had me writhing and yelling out loud. And I hate when that happens.

In the dream I was sleeping in a room where there was a door left open. It was the door to a dark attic and I wanted it closed. But no one would close it for me. I wanted it shut because I was afraid that something would come down the stairs and get me. I tried to call out for help but as is the case with my nightmares, I couldn't get the words out. I was screaming, "Help me! Help me!" I was frozen with fear, watching the attic door for something horrid to appear. Just before it did, one of the monks from the temple rushed into the room to save me. He picked me up out of the bed, brought me to another room with a warm, cozy fireplace and set me up with a comfy blanket on the floor. He lay protectively at a distance to keep an eye on me as I drifted off. I was safe and nothing could harm me.

When I woke up the next morning I felt somewhat bewildered. There was no movement in the dorm room. Since my first night with Jen (who had since gone), four other women had come to stay. I pulled back my privacy blankets to reveal an empty dorm room. All of my roommates were likely at the temple. I looked at my watch. The first session was well underway.

I groaned at my irresponsibility and climbed out of bed. It was snowing heavily outside. With a big yawn I wandered down the stairs into the kitchen where Kay was sitting quietly at the table stirring a cup of tea.

"Did you hear me talking in my sleep last night?" I asked her.

"You know, funny you should ask that. I remember somebody crying and I thought they were saying 'help me, help me', but I didn't think it was you."

"I think it was me. I was having a nightmare," I said.

"About what?" she asked me.

"I'm not really sure," I wondered. "Something in the dark I couldn't see."

Sara the singer walked in at that moment and looked at me concerned.

"Hey there. Are you okay?" she asked me.

"You heard me last night, too?"

"Yeah," she said. "You were crying and you went on for like three minutes, too. I wasn't sure if I should wake you up. It was – awful, actually."

"It was awful and no one woke me up?" I said surprised.

"Well you stopped, eventually." Kay offered.

But I didn't stop. As a matter of fact the entire day was tearful to the point that my eyes burned by the end of it. I went to the second meditation session and decided ten minutes in that I just wasn't ready for it. I needed more sleep, no question. But I sat there anyway. Why? Because we meditated on compassion and it was something I really felt I needed to understand. What I didn't realize was that it was pulling up more hurt from the depths of my heart, ultimately causing me to relive the pain of my recent ill-fated relationship.

Now I should tell you that through every meditation, two people are at the forefront of my mind: my darling Madison-Mae and my former beau. When we meditated on cherishing others, he was there. When we mediated on wishing love and giving, he was there. When we mediated on compassion, he was practically stepping on my feet. I emptied my heart out to him in my mind, crying the entire time. And not like a sappy little child, but like a grieving widow. Emotion just poured out of me: pure, unadulterated, *raw* emotion. I'm willing to bet Gen Kelsang thought I had some serious emotional issues because I was constantly spouting like a broken faucet, all wrapped up in my black scarf.

When the session was over I dragged myself back to the barn and headed for my bed. But when the one and only computer in the house caught my eye, I felt compelled to sit down and check my e-mail. I was hoping to find one from the very man I had meditated on all day. I knew it would be there, too, because there was one in my inbox every single day since my arrival… except for yesterday. But I figured he was busy yesterday. So I really needed to see one today. I needed to read it and to know that he still loved me, despite my chaos. I sat down at the computer, logged on *aaaannnndd* - no e-mail.

My heart sank to my feet. At first I was hurt. Badly. Then I felt anger push the hurt away and take over. And I wasn't just angry, I was downright *pissed*. How could he just throw me aside like that? Sure, I tossed him aside when I broke up with him and asked *him* to move on, but I never really expected him to do the same.

It was only 10 o'clock in the morning when I realized how pissed I really was. How could he just ignore me after everything I had given him? I gave him love. I gave him happiness. Sure, I gave him uncertainty and heartache, but I still gave him peace and stillness, didn't I? He can't drop me one little e-mail? I pushed back the chair, raced upstairs to my bed where I should've been sleeping, grabbed my cell phone, hopped into my car and drove down the road until I found a strong signal for my phone. Then I proceeded to call him over and over and over again, sobbing from the very depths of my heart and even screaming to get the pain out. He didn't answer. He was either sleeping or he had his phone on silent. And so I sat there in my car, cursing him and cursing Buddha and dharma and any other word that ended with an 'a' in the Buddhist culture.

"This crap doesn't work!" I screamed at the top of my lungs. "Look at me! I am a mess! I am a freak-show and a mess!"

I sobbed and sobbed and sobbed. Then I called his number again and left him two absolutely hysterical messages that I'm quite certain would classify me as certifiable if the appropriate doctor heard them. When I felt numb and empty and my head buzzed from screaming I went back to my room and slept.

When I woke up it was about 5 o'clock. I didn't feel any better. However, I did feel like an idiot for leaving such crazy messages on his phone. I felt like I needed to explain myself. So I skipped the last session and got back in my car to drive to the same spot and call him. Much to my surprise, he answered. I apologized profusely and told him the person that left the messages was not me. I explained I felt jaded because I felt I had given him *so much* of my heart during my meditations and all I wanted in return was a simple little e-mail; an acknowledgement that he still cared. But of course he had no idea what I was talking about. He didn't know what I was going through every time I stepped foot in that temple. As far as he was concerned I was sitting next to a statue of a Buddha, seated ever so carefully in the lotus position meditating in pure silence. He didn't know about the different levels of emotion I was pulling up from the depths of my very soul for hours at a time. He knew nothing about it. And he told me that. Of course I understood this. It's not like he was picking up my Buddha frequency.

"I don't know what to say," he said confused. "I'm trying to let go of you but you wont let me."

"That's because I don't know how and I don't want to be alone. I mean, we still love each other, right?"

"I guess," he said.

"Well don't we?" I could feel the mad woman in me rising again.

"We do, yes. That doesn't just go away. But you ended this. You told me to move on and that's what I'm trying to do."

My GOD, did those words break my heart. I imagine it hurt me just as much as the heartache I delivered to him when I ended our relationship two months earlier. It was finally sinking in for me. I knew we weren't meant to be. I had known that for a long time. But I didn't know anything else and *that's* what scared me. I didn't know how to handle my demons and I wanted a love like the kind you read about in fairy tales. I knew I was a mess and my life was a mess and that part of cleaning it up meant getting rid of the dysfunctional relationship that I carried for the past three years. It was no one's fault. We just weren't meant to be. I was finally getting it.

It hurt all the same and so I cried. *Again*. (Because clearly I hadn't cried enough throughout the day.) Through my weeping I told him how sorry I was and that I never meant to hurt him and blah, blah, blah. I cried some more and my eyes were practically bleeding by the time I hung up the phone. I drove back to the temple, wandered aimlessly up the stairs to my bed and fell asleep again. This time I slept firmly through the night.

When I woke up the next morning I seriously considered packing my things and just leaving. It was Tuesday. Which is ironic, because last Tuesday was the day I contemplated leaving, too. I stared at the top of my bunk where I had wedged my bright orange earplugs and grasped at my hair feeling absolutely hopeless.

What was the point of doing this anymore if it didn't even work? Why bother learning how to make peace with others and myself if it turns around and bites me in the back? As I lay there in my little homemade cave feeling all sorts of sorry for myself, I suddenly realized there were people out in the world that had it much worse than me. There were individuals suffering from pain I couldn't even begin to fathom. And me? I'm laying here whining because I don't have someone to love? Seriously? Is that what I'm all whiny about? At least I *had* someone to love. There are folks out there that will never even get to *taste* real love. And hell, I'm not dead yet.

"You idiot," I said out loud. "You're not even giving this a chance. What are you doing? You can't let this jaded love thing bring you down. So what if it didn't work. Move *on*. You have all the resources *right here* to fix everything. Now GET UP. *GET UP* and stop self-cherishing. For God's sake, woman, there are people out there suffering far worse that you can ever imagine. So GET UP!"

And just like that, I did. And I'm glad I did. I marched off to the temple with my heartache lodged firmly in the center of my chest and found my way to my usual chair. I wrapped my big, black scarf around my body and sat up straight, armed with my notebook and a fistful of tissues. No matter what came my way, I would dodge it strategically or face it head on. This was *my* time. *My* life. No one else's. Only *I* had the capacity to change it and make it better. It wasn't up to anyone else. There was no one else I could bring into my life and expect them to mend the fences and make every day sun-shiny. It was all up to *me*. I shook my head at the stupidity I allowed myself to feel for the past several hours. I lifted my head, ready to erase the last few days and focused on Gen Kelsang. He took his seat before us, looking tenderly over the faces that waited eagerly for him to begin. I wondered at that moment if anyone else in the temple felt as twisted and messed up as I did. And if they did, did those feelings dissolve the second that man looked at them? Because they dissolved for me.

"Today," he said in his gentle voice, "we are going to mediate on death and learn how we can find joy in death."

This place never ceases to amaze me.

With his ageless face glowing, he took his long fingers and clenched them into a fist and said, "We are all going to die. Each and every one of us is going to die. It may be years from now, it may be next year. It may even be next week. But it's going to happen. We will leave behind our home, our possessions and our family. So we must learn how to leave this earth without any attachments. We must learn to let go of the material things in our lives that we think are meaningful. Because when we go, we can't take any of it with us."

Joleene DesRosiers Moody

Ah. Attachments. Things we want to keep always. Even the people we love become attachments. Since I've been here, learning the difference between love and attachment has been complicated. But I think I understand it like this:

Love is just that. Love. In love there is no anger. There is no jealousy. In love you accept the person *exactly* as they are and you don't push for them to make change. If and when you experience this kind of unconditional love with somebody, word on the street is that you'll be blown away.

I have spent most of my adult life trying to change the person I was romantically involved with because I couldn't accept them as they were. Take the man I've been bawling over, for example: he used to do this thing where *after* he started his car and it was physically moving down the highway, he would continue to check the ignition to see if the keys were still in it. He would do it at least fifteen times - *while the car was moving.* The wheels are turning and everything, yet every few minutes he would reach his hand up to the steering column to see if they were actually still there. They always were.

This is the same guy that wanted to run an air conditioner on the floor of my bedroom because it wouldn't fit in the window. No matter how hard I tried to tell him that it wasn't safe and he would likely blow us up, he insisted we try it anyway.

"I can't believe you," I told him. "You just don't want to use your head. If the manufacturer wanted us to use it as a floor unit, they would have constructed it as a floor unit. They *sell* floor units. This is not one of them! This unit goes in a window for a reason. You know why? Because it drips water! So lets put it on the floor and turn it on so the water can drip all around it and blow us up."

178

"You are impossible!" he roared at me.

"I'm impossible? You're the guy that runs around the house unplugging appliances when we leave because you're afraid to start a fire - yet you're willing to run a sixty watt air conditioner on *the floor!"*

I couldn't accept him as he was. I couldn't accept anyone I was involved with as they were. I do believe I've driven myself batty in every relationship because of it. I'm not sure if that's because I was never actually in love with any of them, or because I have the patience of a wet mop. In all seriousness though, I now recognize that what I was probably experiencing was merely attachment. Attachment is nothing like love. Attachment is thinking you need someone (or something) to survive. It's dependency. Dependency, by definition, is the state of relying on or being controlled by someone or something else. Correct me if I'm wrong, but that is *not* love. The sad thing is that so many of us will settle for attachment in a relationship just to avoid being alone. We suffer the wrath of the angry and the unhappy in an effort to try to make ourselves happy. The truth of the matter is that we're only making things worse for ourselves.

I know a girl that feels she can't function unless she's with a man. She has to be involved in a relationship or she's miserable. For her the man becomes the source of her happiness. When one relationship fails, she's finds herself another within weeks. She's seen *Sleeping Beauty* and *Cinderella* and believes true happiness begins when the Prince arrives. I'm not criticizing her for this, either, because I've felt the same way. Many of us do. I mean, think about it: when we're *not* involved with someone, we wish we were. We run around all miserable and feeling sorry for ourselves and often end up with low self-esteem because we think we're not good enough to be loved. When we see happy couples giggling together in the mall we just want to trip them or push them over a railing. But when we find that special someone for ourselves, everything changes and suddenly all is right with the world - until the day they try to operate an air conditioner on your bedroom floor.

I refocused on the front of the room where Gen Kelsang continued to talk about love and attachment and how miserable we can end up if we live by attachment. He reminded us that when we die, none of what we have will even matter…not the air conditioner, not the car keys and not the man that constantly reaches for them. Because *nothing* goes with you.

"You must live every day like it's your last. Say to yourself: *I could die today*, and instead of thinking about what you don't have, think about what you do have. Think about the things that bring you joy. Not suffering. Joy. Do you see?"

Do I see? Are you *kidding*? Yes, I see! What a novel way to look at death! What's amazing about this whole concept is that I've heard it all before. I've heard it in conversation. I've heard it in songs and in dialogue between actors in movies. Hell, I've probably said it myself. But it never meant a damn thing to me until now. At that very moment I decided to let go of any anger that I had for anyone in my life. No more would I dwell on the foolish things people did to me. If they wanted to try to hurt me with words or lies, so be it. I would work hard to understand that their anger comes from deep within them and that I have nothing to do with it. It would be tough, but I was willing to try. I didn't want to be mad at anybody anymore. It was a useless, pointless waste of time and energy.

I thought about Maddie again. She wanted a kitty. I had told her no. But you know what, Maddie? If you want a kitty, you got it. You know why? Because I could die tomorrow and never be able to see the joy on your face after bringing that kitty to you.

And another thing: every morning when I wake up I'm going to look my best. When I look good, I feel good. And when I feel good, it's much easier to love myself. I need to love myself. If I can't love who I am, how can I love anybody else?

For the dear man that tried to love me for the past three years, I release you. I respect you enough to let you go so you can find real love. You truly deserve it. Yes, my heart hurts, but you know what? This too shall pass. I will grow form this experience and continue to live. There's so much living to do. I realize heartache is part of the shift, but the longer I dwell in it the more time I waste. I'm going to play outside more with Maddie. I'm going to lay on the beach. I'm going to put all of my pictures in scrapbooks and love my friends like I've never loved them before. I'm going to fall in love with *me* so that I can fall in love with life. I've only got one shot so I need to do it right. No one knows what tomorrow brings, right? So why put myself through such pain when I could be laughing with a friend or playing with my child? Thank you, dharma. (Dharma is the Buddhist practice of living in accordance with a divine will or "goodness".) You're good stuff.

When the teaching was over I wandered quietly into the L shaped café, buried deep in thought. There was so much anger in the world. My mind moved to an incident I had recently been involved in that showed me anger like I'd never experienced it. It was layered, in a sense, and came from the likes of three different people. I was one of them. And it all spun together in the time span of one crazy, hurtful hour.

In 2008 the city of Syracuse tied its record for the number of homicides committed in one year. A double homicide on New Years' Eve brought that number to twenty-five. One of those homicides was a stabbing that

181

took place during a gang fight. A 25-year-old woman unleashed her rage on a 19-year-old woman and stabbed her to death in the stairwell of an apartment building. The following day the 25-year-old suspect was arraigned. I was assigned to shoot the arraignment.

Now I've covered these kinds of stories before and I've seen things get pretty ugly right inside the courtroom. This is often because the attorney representing the suspect almost always, unequivocally, enters a "not guilty" plea on behalf of their client. What many people don't realize is that this is standard courtroom procedure. The justice system says "innocent until proven guilty." So when outraged loved ones hear a cuffed suspect say the words "not guilty", it's not surprising to see one or more jump over the wall of the gallery in an effort to attack the suspect. All hell breaks loose. Knowing this could possibly happen with this case, I asked my supervisor if I could take a photographer with me. He said yes. But the only photographer available at that moment said no. Why? Because the only photographer available at that moment absolutely despised me. I had done something that apparently made him very angry a few months prior – and he had no interest whatsoever in helping me at all.

So I made my way to the courthouse alone, seething with anger at the fact he couldn't set aside his personal feelings for ten minutes and act like a professional.

"That boy needs to grow up," I mumbled to myself as I pulled my camera and tripod out of the truck and made my way up the sidewalk and through the doors of the Onondaga County Courthouse.

The usual photographers from the other television stations were already set up in the hallway, ready to capture the necessary video when the mourning family emerged. Their respective reporters were already inside the courtroom. This angered me even more. As a videojournalist I'm responsible for shooting my own video and conducting interviews simultaneously. I don't have a problem with this. But there are some news stories where a photographer and reporter should team up. This was one of them. I simply couldn't be in two places at once: inside the courtroom to listen to what the judge had to say and *outside* the courtroom to capture video of the emerging family when it was over. I made the logical decision to stay outside the courtroom with my camera ready. It was the lesser of two evils. And here's why: because I can't bring the camera in the courtroom with me, I have to leave it on the floor outside the doors. That means that when the arraignment is over, I have to fight my way through the exiting crowd at warp speed to grab the camera. Then I have to swing it up onto my shoulder, turn it on, wait for the LCD screen to come alive, test the mic levels and white balance the camera so I don't bring back blue, unusable video. Meanwhile, all of the other photographers and reporters are already bombarding the attorneys and family members with questions. I'm still in the corner struggling to find the on switch and set the sound and video levels as quickly as possible without tripping over my mic cord. When I'm finally successful, I've got to shove my way through the other photographers and reporters just to get a comment from whomever it is they've swarmed around. Half the time I'm treated like the runt puppy that can't squeeze in to get a nipple. The rest of the time it's too late and every one has exited the premises with no intention of answering more questions from the last reporter. So, I've learned to stand as a photographer in these situations with my camera on my shoulder and ready.

On this day, myself and three other male photographers stood against the cold tile wall before the giant oak doors to the courtroom. As soon as we saw the big silver handle turn on the doors we became armed and ready. Almost simultaneously, we lifted our cameras up off the floor, situated them just right on our shoulders and hit our record buttons.

Dozens of people filed out, some shouting in anger, others crying hysterically. I stood perfectly still against the cold tile wall, following some of the grieving faces with my camera only. My feet never moved. Only my camera did. As a matter of fact, none of the photographers moved. It's like we instinctively knew it was best not to mingle with this grieving crowd. There are times you chase family down the hall to get a comment and there are times you don't. This was a "don't" time.

The tension that snaked in and around the energized crowd was heavy. I could feel it. As I zoomed in on one of the tearful faces in the crowd, I suddenly felt my body crumple against the wall. Within seconds, my right eye began to throb and the camera that was so steady on my shoulder was now in three pieces on the floor.

What the hell just happened?

"Joleene, are you okay?" someone asked me. "My God, girl, can you see me?"

All I could see was the camera at my feet, broken into three pieces. My glasses were at my feet, too. I reached my hand up to my eye and held it there. It was beginning to swell.

"What happened?" I looked at the face that was now in front of me. It was a court officer.

"Did you see which one it was?" he asked me.

Which one? What?

I lifted my head to see a dozen more faces around me now. A crowd was quickly forming. Somehow I had become the center of attention.

"Sit her down," someone was saying. "Sit her down, she's dizzy!"

"What *happened*?" I asked again.

"Joleene, it's Murray. Can you see my fingers? How many fingers am I holding up?" Murray is a photographer from one of the other television stations.

"Did someone hit me?" I asked him.

"Yes," he said to me. "But they got him."

I looked down the hall where a jumble of activity attracted even more onlookers. Someone was yelling and at least three court officers had a young man up against the cold tile wall and were cuffing him. He couldn't have been more than fifteen years old.

"Hey, Joleene, lift your head up," Murray said. He was looking carefully at my eyes, which were slowly filling with tears. My entire body began to shake. Then my heart began to hurt. That's when my peripheral changed. Not because I had been punched in the head by an angry young man, but because I was no longer looking at someone's pain through the lens of my camera. I had become a part of it. It wasn't just a story anymore. It was reality. And it hit me square in the face. That boy was angry. Not at me, but at life. And death. He was angry because he lost someone he loved in a senseless, tragic way. He couldn't make sense of it. And because he couldn't make sense of it, he struck out. He saw four television cameras lined up neatly in a row and it triggered him. Without a thought he reached out to attack the camera closest to him. That happened to be me. That boy revved up his fist and power housed it into my camera, knocking my head and back hard into the tile wall behind me. I never saw him coming. My focus was to the left. I was completely blind to him as he came at me from the right.

As I sat there waiting for the ambulance that someone had called, I couldn't help but feel for that boy. I rubbed at my heart. The compassion I felt filled my whole chest. The people in front of me, staring down at me, began to blur as tears filled my eyes and streamed down my face.

Why is everyone so angry?

Eventually the crowd dispersed and I was left alone in the hallway with one court attendant until the ambulance arrived. I felt like a fool as they strapped me to the stretcher and carried me out. But they didn't want to take any chances with possible internal injuries. So I let them carry me out, along with my pride, onto one of the more populated street in Syracuse. My eye throbbed with pain and my neck was beginning to stiffen. But it was nothing compared to what I was feeling inside. As the medics pushed me into the rig that would whoosh me off to the hospital, I thought about all of the anger that had swirled into my energy zone in the past hour: the anger the photographer had shown me by refusing to work side by side with me: the anger I felt because he refused: the anger of the people that poured out of the courtroom after the not guilty plea was entered, and the anger of the 15-year-old boy who had just lost his aunt in a senseless act of violence. I realized that at any given moment at just about any place on the map, there is the possibility that anger can erupt and contaminate a circumstance, ultimately affecting a whole group of unsuspecting people almost simultaneously. Anger quickly infects others. And unless an act of love or kindness stops it, the anger will continue to circulate down avenues that feed it and keep pushing it along.

I closed my eyes and took a deep breath. In that instant I realized something quite profound. I didn't belong here anymore. What I was doing wasn't helping people, it was hurting them. It was magnifying their pain and circumstance so others at home eating dinner or running on their treadmill could see what the cruel world outside looked like. And that didn't make me very happy.

Entry #8

Amazing things happen when you least expect it. Sometimes they carry with them a sign. Something amazing happened to me today and when it did, it made me realize the force beyond us where the Divine resides is more than just a story. It is authentic and absolutely real. Whether the Divine is a being of light or the entire Universe matters not; the fact that a collective consciousness is guiding us toward a most remarkable life is certain.

Today we went on a field trip. When I learned that Max from Rochester and Dave from England needed a few items from town, I was tripping over my own two feet to follow them in my car. I had to get a gift for Gen Kelsang. Sara the singer told me it was customary to give your teacher a parting gift. After brainstorming what a simple, peaceful man might want, I decided on some wool socks. Having seen the man's socks everyday for nearly two weeks I felt compelled to find him a nice maroon pair to match his robes. Gen Kelsang's feet might be a size fourteen. They are long and balanced and often covered with grey dress socks. I wanted to put a smile on his face with a nice, cozy, maroon pair.

Kay wanted to tag along and check out the local thrift shop. I wanted to wander through an indoor flea market. We were all about finding hidden treasures in such stores. So off we went to the little city of Port Jervis. Our first stop was the thrift shop. I found two very nice tops for work and paid a dollar for each. Kay found some good deals as well and we left the thrift shop beaming.

"Where did Lhadron say the flea market was?" Kay asked me as we climbed into my car.

Lhadron is one of the nuns at the temple.

"I don't remember," I said.

"She said it was on this same street." Kay was checking both sides of the road as I pulled my car into the flow of traffic.

My mind wasn't so much on the flea market as much as it was visiting Wal-Mart to find some maroon socks. As we drove along Pike Street through Port Jervis past dozens of tiny shops, I looked up on my side of the street and saw the words *FLEA MARKET* out of the corner of my eye. The sign suddenly triggered the memory of a dream I had just weeks prior.

"Kay," I said with excitement, "we have to go in there!"

"We *are* going in there," she said dryly. "That's part of the plan."

"No, you don't understand," I said. "Oh my gosh!"

The dream was coming back to me fast and hard and I couldn't pull over quick enough to get in there.

"What?" she said. "What the hell is wrong with you?"

"I had this dream a while back," I said a bit flustered. "I was at a flea market. Part of it was outside and part of it was inside. I was searching for one of those – screen thingees. Do you know what I'm talking about?"

"No," she said flatly.

"You know, one of those screens? It's usually oriental and you can get dressed behind them or they split a room? You know? One of those?"

"Oh!" she said laughing. "A shoji screen!"

"Yeah!"

I whipped the steering wheel around and looked over my shoulder, still talking excitedly as I manipulated the car neatly against the curb.

"I've wanted one of those screens for some time now," I continued. "I don't know what for but that doesn't really matter right now. In my dream I was searching every aisle and every corner of this particular flea market. I was looking behind antique dressers and all this other crap I can't even begin to describe right now."

Kay's dry, stone face was coming to life. "And?"

"And I wouldn't leave until I found one." I put the car in park and looked at her. "I found one eventually. But I just remember that I wouldn't leave until I absolutely had one in my possession."

"Well we're gonna go right after we get back from Wal-Mart."

"But I just parked. We have to go in now!" I said pointing to the flea market.

"Can't," she said. "Sign says closed for lunch."

And it did. Scrawled on brown cardboard with a black sharpie the sign read, *Out To Lunch. Back in an Hour.*

"We'll come back," she said patting me on the knee.

"We have to," I said. "I mean, that dream just came to me as soon as I saw the flea market. That's my gut talking, right? Telling me to go in?"

"I would say it is some sort of intuition, yes."

"Can you imagine?" I said daydreaming a little. "If it's in there, I'll *die!*"

Admittedly, I was a little dramatic about the moment. But that's because I was feeling a "pull" within me. It was strong and I wanted to see what it was all about. I bit my tongue and pulled back into traffic.

We found our way to Wal-Mart and were a bit shell shocked when we walked through the front doors. The bright, florescent lights were *too* bright and there were people everywhere. After being stowed away at the quiet, peaceful temple, the noise of the outside world had me feeling slightly left of center.

"Excuse me," one lady in a fluffy orange coat said rudely as she zipped past us to get outside. "Maybe you shouldn't be standing in the doorway? Doesn't seem like the smartest move in the world," she crabbed.

I turned to watch her waddle out the door with her overloaded cart.

Dave from England said it would feel different when we stepped back into the "real" world. The faces of people I generally ignore were all I could look at now. Some were angry, others seemed lost in thought. All of them were in a hurry.

"These are the faces of the suffering," I could hear Gen Kelsang say in my head. "These are the people of the world that can't be still. They don't love themselves very much."

The feeling was a bit overwhelming and rather raw. As we walked toward where we thought the sock aisle would be, I looked closely at every face that passed me. What were some of these people thinking that they looked so full of angst? One man walked past us dragging his very upset child by her arm. He looked like he was ready to step off the edge and not think twice about the fall. I shook my head and tried to refocus. What did I come in here for? Socks. And drain stoppers. Dave said the kitchen needed drain stoppers. So why were we standing in the toy aisle?

"Can I help you two ladies?" A rather jovial employee in a blue smock asked us. We didn't answer him right away so he said with a laugh, "You two look like a couple of lost souls."

My eyes widened at his comment because he was dead on and didn't even realize it. Here we were, two young women struggling with finding our place in life, not quite grounded and soul-searching every corner of our being every second of every hour. We chose to spend time among the most peaceful people in the world in a tiny corner of New York State in an effort to find tranquility and elude suffering, and here comes this guy with a big smile and three stars on his name tag, telling us we look like two lost souls.

"You have no idea," I said smiling at the man. He nodded, looking at both of us with his hands on his hips.

"We need drain stoppers," Kay said to him.

"Well you're not gonna find 'em among the Barbie dolls! Other side of the store. Aisle twelve."

I thanked him. He saluted us and walked away. Kay's jaw was on the floor.

"Can you believe that just happened?" she said.

"What?"

"We *do* look like two lost souls because we *are* two lost souls and he comes up and tells us that we look like two lost souls. Do you see the spiritual irony here?"

"I do," I said smiling.

"It's like – he *knew*."

"He didn't know," I said, a bit more in tune with the moment. "But it's profound to us because we're beginning to understand things about us we didn't understand before. We're seeing ourselves in these people."

When you spend the majority of your day meditating, looking for a place of solace, statements like that from the little, round Wal-Mart guy can be eye-opening. It's a tribute to self-realization, really. When you learn to recognize your own suffering and the suffering that unfolds around you, it truly is an awakening. Strangely, you find yourself embracing the notion that there is a way to live a more calming life. When you can identify with the pain that rattles within you and recognize that you can do something about changing it and removing it, you're on your way to freedom.

We bring on our own suffering in so many ways. Usually it's because we go on relentlessly with needless thinking. It can happen when someone rejects us. When they make us feel less than stellar, we tend to think what they say is true and then curl up in a little ball feeling all sorts of sorry for ourselves.

He said I'm an idiot, therefore I am.

She said I'm fat, therefore I am.

They said I'm worthless, therefore I must be.

No. You're not.

Gen Kelsang's teachings echoed in my head and I thought: *We can't let others degrade us or make us feel small. We create our own self-worth, not those around us. We need to find our beauty and embrace it.*

It may take time to discover that you are worthy of just as much love and respect as anyone else. But you will soon see it. It took you years to feel the way you do about who you are now. It's going to take a few more to turn that around.

After walking aimlessly through the aisles searching for sink drains and size fourteen maroon socks, we left the store empty handed. No drains, no socks. But our adventure was far from over.

We met Max and Dave in an even brighter hardware store where drains were aplenty. (No socks, of course.) I didn't want to leave town without a gift for Gen Kelsang and was a bit torn when we left the hardware store.

"You'll find something, chicken," Dave said. "And if you don't, Gen Kelsang isn't going to think twice about it. Maybe you'll find something at the flea market."

"Really?" I scoffed. "Something used?"

"He doesn't care. It's not about the quality, don't you see? It's about giving. Haven't you learned anything here?" he asked me gently.

"Yeah. Stay away from brightly lit stores and guys with big smiley faces on their vests."

He didn't know what that meant.

"Listen," I said, "we're going to the flea market now. Why don't you and Max come with us?"

"No," he said tossing the bag of drains in the back of the Toyota. "Gotta get back and make a meal for the lot of ya."

He kissed me on the forehead and gave us both a wave as he and Max drove away. Kay was standing next to me chomping loudly on her gum.

"We goin'?" she asked me.

"Oh, yes," I said, watching the Toyota move on down the road.

She turned to me with her arms crossed.

"Hey - if that thing is in there, that shoji screen, I don't know - that would be *so* intense."

As much as I would have liked my dream to come true I also knew the possibility of it was slim. Granted, it would be a magical feeling if I were to walk in there and find one. But we're in a tiny city the size of my thumb. What are the chances?

The air outside was cold and bitter and I was frozen to the bone. My shoes were wet and I had foolishly left my coat behind. I barely warmed up in the car on the short drive back to Pike Street where the flea market awaited us. The out to lunch sign was gone and replaced with: *Hours: 11-6. No one under 22 allowed inside. If questionable, you will be ID'd.*

Well, I've got that one covered. I'm over twenty-two. If they were to ask for my ID however, I certainly wouldn't complain. But they didn't. As a matter of fact the two workers behind the counter didn't even acknowledge us when we walked in.

The store itself was dimly lit and much more digestible than the screaming reality of Wal-Mart. A dated transistor radio played quietly in a corner. There was so much stuff to look at, I didn't know where to start. The shelves in front of us were packed to the hilt with mismatched glasses and plates and various statues made of plastic or wood. Kay headed straight into the first aisle. I stood there for a moment, not sure which direction to go. A feeling of uncertainty filled my gut and I sighed heavily. I know this feeling; it's the feeling of being lost and unclear. I remember experiencing it several times after I first came home from college and was staying with my father. I used to go for a walk every day. There were some days I would walk aimlessly throughout the neighborhood with my mind moving at ten thousand miles an hour. I would walk with my brain churning until I happened upon an intersection. And then I would stand there, looking down all four roadways, trying to decide which way to go. It wasn't a light debate, either. It was huge. I would stand in the street, lined with quaint houses and sturdy sidewalks, completely indecisive as to which way to go. I couldn't make up my mind. Straight? Left? Right? Back the way I came? That tiny, insignificant decision would stop me dead in my tracks in the middle of a sunny afternoon. I was so afraid that making a wrong turn would be detrimental. In what way, I didn't know. And as I stood in the middle of the store today, hearing only the sound of the crackling transistor radio, I felt that very same feeling. I shook my head to erase the memory and took a deep breath.

Just go.

Without a second thought I headed to my left into a separate room.

Wow, I thought as I looked around me. There was so much *stuff!* I started in the corner by the entrance and looked at everything. I mean *everything*. Every little detail on every piece of merchandise. There were chairs and tables and totem poles (Really? Totem poles?) stacked high to the ceiling. There were old trunks and wall hangings and chairs and toys. Nothing was ordinary. Everything was unique. More pictures and a guitar and three bras for ten dollars and *more* totem poles and beautiful cedar chests. A small corner stuffed to the brim didn't reveal what I was looking for, nor did the smaller room beyond that. I turned around and walked back the way I came, again passing the chairs and the bras and the totem poles when I turned around to take one more look overall and almost dropped to my knees. There, on the wall to the entrance of the second room, was a shoji screen. It was neatly folded and leaning quietly against the wall.

My jaw dropped. Just like in the movies. It literally dropped.

No way.

I felt my heart-strings tighten and my hands began to shake as I walked toward it. Somehow I missed it completely when I first came in. As a matter of fact, I was standing right next to it when I stopped to look at an assortment of books stuffed in a corner. How could I have missed it? It stood at least seven feet tall, was a light to medium wood color and etched with simple trees and birds.

I don't believe this, I thought as I reached out to touch it. My whole body lit up as the dream came back to me. Tears filled my eyes and I laughed at the sight of it. My shaking hands worked to open the panels, revealing more etched drawings of people. The piece was large and awkward and there had to be at least ten panels, total.

Kay. Where was Kay? I needed her. She *had* to see this. I quickly dashed out of the room and re-entered the main part of the store. She was browsing a shelf overflowing with cheaply painted nick-knacks.

"Hey!" I whispered loudly.

She looked up at me.

"It's here!"

"No," she mouthed, her eyes suddenly as big as quarters.

"Yes!" I said waving her toward me. "Come see!"

She stood there with her jaw dropped, a porcelain Bo-Peep clutched tightly in her right hand.

Come see!" I said again.

I smiled and turned on my heel. I could hear her moving quickly behind me as she followed me to the other room.

"Oh my gosh!" she shouted as we approached it. "Have you opened it yet? You have to open it!"

"I know, I know! I only opened one panel. It's heavy. I mean look at the size of this thing!"

"Stand there," she said pointing to a spot on the floor, "and we'll pull it out together."

She grabbed the outer panel and motioned for me to get out of the way. As she struggled with the weight of the other panels, I hopped in next to her. Slowly, we opened the great shoji to reveal what was etched inside. And if you want to talk about being blown away, this was the moment that really knocked me on my feet: panel one and two opened to reveal a temple. Panels three and four were that of a man meditating. The rest of the screen unfolded to reveal an entire scene of serenity including a pathway, a happy dog and three Buddha's making soup. There was another man reading a book and yet another with fruit offerings for the statue before him and all of this was etched in the compassionate color of maroon. Kay and I were speechless.

"No way," she said flatly.

I couldn't talk because tears were streaming down my face. I was quite certain if this whole crying business kept up my face was going to melt off. Talk about karma and living within a dream! Not only did I find a shoji in a flea market, I found a shoji in a flea market that represented the very life I was living at that very moment in time.

"I have to have this," I said to her.

"This is amazing," she said, shaking her head. "Utterly amazing. What are you thinking right now?"

I couldn't even explain to her what I was thinking because I didn't really know. Yes, I was amazed. But at what? This wasn't just irony or coincidence. My heart and gut were on fire with a feeling I can only equate to love. I felt an overwhelming joy. I felt a bliss that was better than anything I had ever felt before.

"I want to feel like this all the time," I said to her through my blubbering. "Can you sense how I feel right now?"

She laughed and pulled at my arm.

"C'mon. Let's go buy it," she said.

And so I did.

The little guy behind the counter graciously carried the awkward piece out to my car with the help of two younger men from the store. Kay and I shoved the front passengers seat as far forward as possible and pushed both back seats down. I popped the trunk open. We watched helplessly as the trio of men tried to maneuver the giant piece through the trunk and into the backseat. It wouldn't fit.

"It ain't goin' in," the little guy said.

"It has to," I told him. "I live almost five hours away. Can we tie it to the top of my car instead?"

"Are you kidding me?" he asked. "You'll cave the roof! This thing has gotta weigh over two hundred pounds."

"We've got to get Dave back here with the Toyota," I said to Kay. And then to the little guy, "Can I keep it here until tomorrow?"

"Yeah, sure, I don't care."

And that was that.

"How are you going to get it home?" Kay asked me as we climbed into my car to head back to the temple.

"I don't know," I said honestly. "Maybe Dave has the answer."

****

"You have to leave it here," Dave said when we got back to the kitchen. "Which means you'll have to come back to the temple another time with a bigger vehicle. Have you got a truck?"

"I know where I can get one," I said.

"Okay," he said. "Come back again. That's all."

We had pushed the tables and chairs aside in the dining room to set the screen up and take a good, hard look at it. It was dark now, and the dim lights in the dining room kept us from really seeing the full beauty of my new treasure.

"Let's use this lamp to shine it on each panel so we can see the details better," Max from Rochester said.

He was holding a tall, black office lamp under his arm. I watched as he plugged it into the wall. He tipped it ever so carefully so the top of the lamp was facing the screen.

"Wow," I said. "Look at the detail on this thing."

"It's of Buddhist nature," Dave said. "Do you see that, chicken? Tibetan, I think. Look at all the Buddha's.

199

Each one is doing something different." He looked up at me with a smile. "I don't think this was an accident, you finding this."

"I second that," Kay said moving closer to the etchings. "Do you see the significance of this thing? Every action etched on this screen illustrates this place."

"What do you mean?" Dave asked her.

"Look here. The dog. That's Zeus – the dog here at the temple. And over here? The three monks making soup? That's Dave and Max and Mikyopa, the monk that does all the cooking. Over here is someone reading a book. Joleene, that's you. And here is a pathway, right? That's the pathway behind the temple."

"The one I went on with Kevin," I said.

"Yes! And look at the temple. It's so similar to the temple here. Joleene, Dave is right. This was meant to be for you. This is a gift."

I nodded in agreement as I continued to study the etchings on the shoji. My heartstrings were still very tender from the original discovery of my treasure just hours before. Somebody or something was trying to talk to me, to tell me something, to send me a message. My emotions were stirred up, certainly, but not in a way that wasn't unpleasant or dissatisfying. I felt very much at peace and was grateful for the good energy around me.

It's these kinds of feelings that make me want to stay at the temple for a long, long time. But my time here is coming to an end. I only have two more days left. On Sunday I'll have to pack my things and go. My bed will go back in my trunk and my few belongings to the back seat. The shoji will have to stay behind until I can come back again. And yes, I will come back again.

Entry #9

Today I go home.

I spent my last few days here at Kadampa weeding out my soul. I made new friends and have adopted a new way of learning how to live. I will take with me what I have learned and I will work on loving who I am every day.

Suma, the nun who urged me to stay two weeks ago, gave me some elements so that I can build a shrine of my own at home.

"Your shrine will create itself," she said to me, closing my hand around a little pewter Buddha statue. "You'll see."

Amazingly, it did. Between parting gifts and tidbits I picked up at the Kadampa bookstore, I ended up with every tool necessary to build my shrine. The only thing I was missing was a gift to leave with Gen Kelsang. On my last day I approached him.

"Can I have a word?" I asked him as the dining room buzzed with hungry people. It was lunchtime.

"Of course," he said to me.

I expected to chat with him right there on the spot but he turned toward the staircase that led to his chambers. I humbly followed him. When we entered his room, he sat quietly in the same chair where he had sipped his soup just two weeks before.

"I am told," I said nervously, "that I should have a parting gift for you. But I have nothing."

He smiled at me.

"I actually tried to find you some warm, maroon colored socks, but I didn't have any luck," I said.

"I have something for you," he said, reaching for the top of the dresser behind him. He brought down a book, nestled comfortably in a handmade silk book cover.

"You will be well," he said handing me the book. "That is your gift to me. That you will be well."

My heart filled with the same kind of joy I felt just a few days before I found my dream treasure.

"Thank you," I said as I stood to go. He bowed before me, his long hands clasped together in gratitude. I did the same, feeling whole and pure.

And that was that.

I said good-bye to my new friends and good-bye to my shoji screen that temporarily stood in a corner of the dining room. With a heavy heart, I trudged through the snow back to the barn and up the stairs where my bag and comforter and pillow awaited. Most of the retreat students had gone already. Only one train for New York City departed on this Sunday, and many of those that stayed at the temple were city residents. But not me. I was five hours from my little apartment and my little girl. I was also in no particular hurry to get back. But alas, I had to make tracks sooner than later in order to get home at a decent hour.

I dragged my bag and bedding down the stairs and into the kitchen. A warm cup of tea to go would make the trip. I would miss the aroma of the little kitchen, which often smelled like raisin toast and peanut butter. I steeped the tea with tenderness, thinking of how fond I had grown of drinking it these past few weeks. Once the brew was finished, I poured it into my to-go cup and headed toward the door. There, on the seat next to the door was my fleece pullover. I grabbed it and tucked it under my arm. Then, off I went to start my car and scrape the ice from it to prepare for the long journey back home.

Once the ice was scraped from the outside of my vehicle and the heat had penetrated and warmed the inside, I hopped into the drivers seat and proceeded to do what I do best: cry. I put the car in reverse and ambled down the driveway toward the bumpy, stone road where the wild turkeys were fluttering. My tears weren't tears of sadness. They were tears of joy. I realized I had done something significant for my soul by spending an extended period of time at the Kadampa Meditation Center. I had fallen in love. I drove away with a strong determination to never look back at who I was when I arrived. I thought of Dave as I pulled out onto the main road and cried even harder. We had shared several talks at night over tea. I didn't write about them, but I suppose that's because he took up my writing time by yapping at me all night. Nonetheless, I learned that he, too, suffered hardship. We bonded quite well, as a matter of fact. There was something amazing about that man. Perhaps it was knowing he had stumbled and fallen just like I had – but got right back up to keep moving forward. He would tell me later that we must have known each other in a past life because our karma was so strong. I'm pretty sure he's right.

My overdrawn sobbing made me laugh and I reached for the little black button on my door to crack the window for a bit of air. Just as my finger touched the button, I remembered too late that the window was broken. But the damage was done. The glass fell at an angle about an inch or so down into the doorway, leaving a triangle gap that allowed the bitter cold air to whoosh it's way throughout the inside of my car. Because the glass had fallen off the tracking mechanism, using the little black button to try and roll the window back up was futile. Smiling at a situation I would normally curse at, I looked around my car for something to stuff into the gap. My fleece was next to me on the passengers seat. I grabbed the piece of clothing, ready to stuff it in the gap when a hand towel from the barn kitchen fell into my lap. I had inadvertently picked up one of the towels when I picked up my fleece! Stealing is certainly not tolerated in a place as wonderful as Kadampa. The Buddha's could demerit one for such an act. But as soon as that thought arose, it disappeared with a giggle and tears of joy came again. Despite the fact I was leaving meditation center, it clearly wasn't going to leave me.

I picked up the towel and stuffed it in the crack of the broken window.

I was warm again.

BIBLIOGRAPHY

Brown, Les. *The Revolution Within: Conference*. Utah, Audio, circa 1994.

Browne, Malcolm W. *Signal Travels Farther and Faster Than Light*. Thomas Jefferson National Accelerator Facility, 2007. Print

Campbell, Thomas. *My Big Toe: A trilogy Unifying Philosophy, Physics and Metaphysics*. USA: Lightning Strike Books, 2003. Print.

Hay, Louise. *You Can Heal Your Life, the movie*. Hay House Incorporated, 2007. Video

Lesser, Elizabeth. *Broken Open*. USA: Villard Books, 2004. Print.

McCourt, Frank. *We All Can Have Second Acts (& Third!)* Parade, 2008. Print.

Millman, Dan. *The Life You Were Born to Live: A Guide to Finding Your Life Purpose*. Novato, CA: New World Library, 1993. Print.

Nichols, Lisa. *No Matter What!* New York: Hachette Book Group, 2009. Print.

Schuman, Helen and William Thetford. 1976. *A Course In Miracles*. Mill Valley, CA: Foundation for Inner Peace, 2007. Print.

Tolle, Eckhart. *The Power of Now*. Novato, CA: New World Library, 1999. Print.

Tolle, Eckhart. *Living a Life of Inner Peace*. Novato, CA: New World Library, 2004. Audio.

Wattles, Wallace. *The Science of Being Great*. 1911. Radford, VA: Wilder Publications, 2008. Print.